WRITING SCARY SCENES

by

RAYNE HALL

CONTENTS

INTRODUCTION

I love scaring readers. Don't you?

This book will teach you practical tricks for turning up the suspense. Make your readers' hearts hammer with terror, their breaths quicken with excitement and their skins tingle with goosebumps of delicious fright.

Are you working on a ghost story, a horror novel, a thriller, a paranormal romance, an urban fantasy or a romantic suspense? Whether you're planning or revising your scary scenes, whether you aim to tease your readers with mild tension or to send them on a rollercoaster ride of fear, this book shows step-by-step how to create the effects you want.

I never meant to become a horror author. As a novice writer, I fluttered from genre to genre, penning everything from funny poems to tragic love stories – but the stories that won contest prizes were always the scary ones, and most of the yarns accepted for publication were horror.

I set about mastering the craft of scary writing by studying the masters, authors who treat their readers to first-rate fear: Edgar Allan Poe, Ray Bradbury, E.F. Benson, Shirley Jackson, Stephen King, Lisa Gardner, Tanith Lee and many more. I studied their techniques, practised them and added them to my own writing craft toolkit.

My fiction has become better. When I look at a story I wrote years ago, I see at a glance what needs changing to turn up the fear. Other writers and publishers come to me for help. I offer freelance consulting, teach classes on how to write scary scenes, edit anthologies of horror fiction and continue to write my own scary tales.

Whenever I try to write something different, the story quickly turns into something dark and scary.

a guilty secret, and the housekeeper was on a serial killing spree. I just could not keep the horrors out of the book.

Another time, I conceived an adventure fantasy about a swashbuckling hero who fought evil... but as I wrote, it turned out that the evil he was fighting was inside him. The book quickly filled with war, rape, torture, demonic possession and human sacrifice.

Clearly, I'm meant to write dark and scary stuff.

My preference is for horror without much violence - no chainsaw massacres, no dismembered bodies, no lakes of blood or mounds of gore. Although I've written scenes of torture and mutilation, my preference is for psychological horror. I like observing how characters feel and act in the face of fear, and I want my readers to share that experience. Often, the characters in my stories have brought the fate upon themselves, or the boundaries between good and evil are blurred. What is more scary than our own evil side?

Whatever kind of fear you want to create – with or without gore, psychological or graphic, mild or intense – this book will show you how.

Most of these techniques will suit many different scenes, but you may choose to use some and discard others. You're the CEO of your writing; your vision counts. Choose the techniques which suit the story you're working on and your individual author's voice. You can dip into and out of this book, picking up the skills you need right now, and leave others for a future project.

Writing Scary Scenes is a book for advanced-level and professional writers. It equips authors who have already mastered their craft with specialist skills. If you're a beginner, I recommend you start with a book on the basics of fiction writing.

when talking about characters, I'll switch between "he" and "she". Everything I say applies regardless of gender.

I hope you'll enjoy my book and will apply the techniques to your own writing. Create scenes which are so suspenseful, so exciting, so scary that they stay in your readers' mind. Scaring readers is fun!

Rayne Hall

CHAPTER 1: FLAVOURS OF FEAR

When you write in a deep point of view (PoV), the character's emotions transfer to the reader. By scaring the PoV character, you will scare the reader.

Usually, you want the reader to feel what the protagonist feels. Sometimes it's different. For example, you may want the reader to feel suspense and apprehension about something the protagonist isn't aware of. She's blithely taking off her clothes on the beach and stepping into the sea for a swim when the reader already knows – but she doesn't – that the water is full of sharks.

Fear comes in many different flavours. For each scene you write, choose one or several kinds of fear.

SUSPENSE

This is the urge to find out what will happen next, or how it will happen. It drives the reader to turn the pages. Sometimes, the reader feels suspense before the PoV does. Suspense makes the heart beat faster, and the person may sit on the edge of their seat, leaning forward.

Readers love suspense. Whatever genre you write, create a lot of suspense throughout your book, but vary its intensity.

UNEASE

This is a mild form of fear. The character doesn't know whether there is any danger or what kind, she just has a niggling feeling that something is wrong.

cross and uncross repeatedly, though she may not be aware that they do. Perhaps she paces up and down the room, checks her appointment diary frequently without really looking at it, or picks the varnish off her fingernails. If other people are around, she may pretend not to notice that something is amiss. Her dialogue may become stilted. If she's having a meal, she may have no appetite and push the food around on her plate. She may tell herself that there's nothing wrong, and force her limbs to relax.

This type of fear suits every genre, and you can use it several times in your book. Often, unease is followed by stronger forms of fear when the danger manifests.

ANXIETY

This is similar to unease, but the character knows the danger is real. This is what people feel before important job interviews, before a bungee jump and while sitting in the dentist's waiting room. In fiction, your character may feel this when she is about to enter the monster's lair or when she knocks on the villain's door.

The heart beats fast. The character crosses and uncrosses her legs, adjusts her shirt-cuffs frequently, plays with the necklace at her throat or picks the varnish off her nails, though she may not be aware that she is doing these things. She may hold her palms on her thighs, or rub them together. She may run the fingertips of one hand across the palm of the other, or interlace her fingers and rub them up and down.

Her breathing is shallow. She may feel a strangling pressure on her throat or get mild stomach cramps, and she may need to go to the toilet to relieve her bladder.

constantly doing something with her fingers.

The PoV character's anxiety usually creates suspense in the reader. Don't draw out the anxious phase too long, however, or the character will come across as a wimp.

APPREHENSION

Closely related to suspense, unease, dread and anxiety, this is a mild form of fear. The character knows what menace to expect, but doesn't know yet if it will happen.

The heart beats fast, the breathing is shallow. She may stand with her hands clasped behind her back or sit with her ankles locked around each other. Her scalp prickles and her skin crawls. Her attention is focused and she hears every sound acutely.

You can use this several times in your novel.

FOREBODING

The character senses that something bad is going to happen, but does not yet know what. He may be reluctant to mention his foreboding to others for fear of ridicule.

There's a sensation of heaviness in the stomach, the head or the heart. The throat feels dry, the breathing may become slow and shallow, and there may be a faint tremor in the hands or the voice.

Readers enjoy sharing a PoV's foreboding, but use this emotion sparingly or it loses impact. The best place to insert foreboding is the scene before the terrible event happens.

control over what happens. His heart beats quickly and his senses are heightened. He talks and walks fast, and he may jump up and down or bounce on his seat. If joy outweighs the fear, he may feel a warm glow spreading through his body, but if the fear is stronger than the joy, he may feel cold, especially in his fingers.

Other people note his rapid movements, his fast speech, his flushed face and his shiny eyes.

In the early parts of the novel, the hero often feels excitement when he embarks on his quest. He laughs at warnings, because the risks are worth taking. Later in the story, he'll realise how naïve he was, but it's a good feeling while it lasts.

Excitement suits every genre, and it is most readers' favourite feeling. If you can make the reader share the PoV's excitement, you have them completely.

DREAD

The character and the reader know that a terrible thing is about to happen, but they don't know its exact nature.

The throat is dry, the heart hammers fast, the chest may feel as if all the air is getting squeezed out of it. Arms are hunched close to the body, hands held to the face. The character may bite his nails or dig the nails of one hand into the palm of the other, and he may be reluctant to look in his companions' eyes.

Others watching him see a pale face, perhaps beaded with sweat.

This flavour of fear works especially well in thrillers and horror fiction.

it no more.

The heart races, the knees quake, the throat constricts, and the insides turn to water. The character may feel paralysed, unable to move, run, talk or scream... however much he wants to. The breathing becomes shallow, and he may scarcely dare to breathe.

Terror heightens the senses. He may hear, see, smell and feel things he would not normally notice. At the same time, he may not notice what else is going on around him, because terror drives out all other awareness of reality. He may feel he's being stalked or watched. He may have the urgent need to empty his bladder.

Use terror sparingly, perhaps only once in the book. Terror can last for several minutes, but after that, its symptoms vanish. Bear this in mind when writing your scene: If you keep up the terror non-stop, after a while, the reader won't feel it any more.

Terror is an excellent flavour for horror and thrillers. It can also be good for urban fantasy, but for many other genres, it is too intense.

REVULSION

Revulsion combines the feeling of fear with that of loathing. The character recoils from what he sees. His hand covers his mouth. He swallows a lot although the swallowing feels uncomfortable. He may gag, or his stomach may heave.

He won't touch the object or the person. His first response may be to spin on his heel or turn away, and he'll probably have the urge to leave the room or flee the scene. If the revulsion is caused by another character, he may step back, answer evasively, hold a bag or jacket towards them – as if blocking them – and avoid touching them.

If other people watch him they see a pale face with flat eyes and a curling lip.

The best way to achieve revulsion is by mentioning or describing bad smells. Use this sparingly, however, because readers don't enjoy revulsion as much as they enjoy other flavours of fear. If you write horror fiction, you can use revulsion several times in each novel. In other genres, use it only once or twice – or not at all. Keep it short: one sentence is often enough.

SHOCK

This emotion is similar to dread, but it starts suddenly. It can continue for a while. The character probably makes a small sound – a gasp, yelp or squeal - and then goes silent. If she talks, her voice is low, halting, shaky. She may hold a hand near her throat, but without pressure, or she may pull a bag or other object tightly against her chest, or perhaps she clings to another person for support. The stomach feels heavy, the skin tingles. She probably feels disoriented, though she may also feel euphoric, dizzy or angry.

If other people watch her, they see wide staring eyes (perhaps shiny with tears), pale sweat-beaded skin and a shaky gait.

Shock suits all genres, but it's probably best to use it only once in each novel to avoid boring the reader.

PANIC

Panic is brief and intense. The heart thuds so wildly, it feels like it's about to burst out of the chest. Breathing is rapid. The character has the urgent need to gasp for air, and may feel like she isn't getting enough of it. She also has the urge to leave the place, to get out of the room, to escape. Rational reasoning is impossible.

She probably sweats profusely. She may be shaking uncontrollably. There may be pain in the chest, lungs or throat. She may cling to a railing, an object, a wall, or another person, and may refuse to let go – or she may hug her arms tightly around herself and back away when someone else gets near. She may hyperventilate, drawing in deep, desperate breaths. Panic can lend unaccustomed strength, so in her desperate need to get away, she may be able to break down doors and knock down people who get in her way. While the panic lasts, the character may not feel pain and may be unaware of her injuries.

If someone else watches her, they may see her gasping, sweating, moving in rapid jerking steps and looking wild.

It lasts only for seconds, a couple of minutes at the most. Then it subsides, leaving the character feeling shaky and disoriented. Sometimes, panic ends with the person fainting from panic-induced breathing problems (hyperventilation or a lack of oxygen).

During the short time the panic lasts, your character may do something stupid, such as run away from the panic-causing menace into a much greater danger. This is useful for fiction plots.

It may be best not to use panic more than once in the novel, otherwise your characters may come across as wimps.

Some people suffer from frequent panic attacks and prolonged anxiety as symptoms of a mental health problem. They are usually aware of what is happening and have learnt to gain some control over the panic, for example, by abdominal breathing. However, writing fiction from the point of view of a mentally ill person requires special plotting techniques beyond the scope of this book.

HORROR

This is an intense emotion. It is similar to terror, but the character has more awareness of other realities and more control over his actions, and he can usually move and talk. Often, there's a layer of revulsion. The senses may be dulled.

The heart thuds wildly, sweat runs from the character's forehead and armpits, the palms are moist. The character may speak loudly to cover up his own fear.

Horror doesn't last long, but it can recur.

Depending on the genre, you can add this flavour to several scenes.

CHAPTER 2: INSTANT HOOKS

To keep the reader on the edge of her seat from the beginning to the end of the scene, all you need is one sentence.

This sentence needs to state the scene goal, i.e. what the main character wants to achieve in this scene.

<u>Examples</u>

Lara had to find a way through the labyrinth.

Henry needed to get into the office undetected.

She had to rescue the prince from the dragon's clutches.

I needed to prove my courage to the gang.

I wanted to impress George with my abseiling (American: *"rapelling")*
skills.

He had to sail across the storm-tossed lake.

"I will kill the monster," Mary promised, *"or die trying."*

"Please let me pass," Michael pleaded. *"I must find my sister before she*
dies."

The words *want, need, have to* or *must* are useful in this sentence.

Place this sentence as early as possible in the scene. Sometimes, you can even make it the scene's first sentence.

You may have heard the advice "Show, don't tell." This is a valid recommendation, but don't be afraid to "tell" the goal. You'll do a lot of "showing" in your scary scene. A little "telling" now and then can be effective.

If the reader already knows what the scene goal is (because it's been mentioned in a previous scene), you can state it again, in different words.

MOTIVATION

In addition to stating the scene goal, you may want to state the motivation (the reason why the protagonist needs to achieve the scene goal). What would be the dire consequences of failure? This lends importance to the scene goal.

<u>Examples</u>

I needed to prove my courage to the gang so they would accept me as a member.

Michael had to find his sister, because he was the only one who could heal her poisoned wounds.

If she failed, the only heir to the throne would perish, and the kingdom would erupt in civil war.

TIME LIMIT

For extra suspense, give the protagonist a limited time in which to achieve the goal. This adds urgency and tension.

<u>Examples</u>

Michael had to reach his sister before the poison killed her.

Bianca needed to find the vampires' lair before darkness fell.

He had to disable the bomb before it exploded at half past two.

In Chapter 8 (*Keep the Clock Ticking*) we'll look at this technique in greater depth.

OBSTACLES

You may add a mention of obstacles which stand between the protagonist and the goal, especially dangers and threats.

Example

He had to cross the storm-tossed lake, but the boat was leaking, and the water was infested with man-eating eels.

This increases the suspense enormously. However, what the protagonist encounters during the scene has to be even more dangerous than what he expects at the outset, so don't reveal too much.

REMIND THE READER

If you state the scene goal at the beginning of the scene, the reader will be hooked and stay hooked, eagerly reading on to find out whether the protagonist achieves it.

At several points during the scene, remind the reader of the scene goal (in different words), to keep the suspense up.

DRAWBACKS

Does this technique have disadvantages? Only one: Like everything, it can become tedious if overused. If every scene in the novel starts with the scene goal in the first sentence, the effect wears off. You can use a scene goal in every scene, but vary its placement, e.g. sometimes in the first paragraph, sometimes in the second, sometimes in the third.

CHAPTER 3: WHAT LURKS BEHIND THAT DOOR?

Here's a quick trick for increasing the suspense: Let your protagonist walk through a doorway on her way to danger.

A PSYCHOLOGICAL TRICK

Film makers use this technique frequently. Next time you watch a thriller, cop drama or horror movie, observe how the camera lingers on the door before the hero enters. Subconsciously, the viewer perceives the door as a barrier: if the protagonist crosses it, she is entering a danger zone. The viewer screams inwardly "Don't open that door!" Of course, the protagonist opens it and enters. By now, the viewer is sitting on the edge of her chair, frightened on the hero's behalf, needing to find out what happens next.

You can use the same trick in your writing: put a door between your protagonist and the danger, and linger for a moment before she or he enters. Any kind of door serves: a front door, a garden gate, a gatehouse, a trap door, a stile, a cave mouth, even a gap in a hedge. This works whether your heroine is a police officer on her way to confront a serial killer, or a governess tempted to explore the mansion cellar's secrets, whether your hero accidentally stumbles into a lair of werewolves or whether he gets dragged into the torture dungeon.

Slow the story's pace for a moment and linger at the door. Describe the door: Is it dark oak, grimy glass, gleaming steel, or splintering hardwood with peeling paint? Are there any danger clues, such as knife marks, smashed glass, ominous stains, thorny plants, perhaps even a sign "Visitors Unwelcome" or "Keep Out" nailed to the centre?

Describe the sound of the doorbell, or the weight of the keys in her hand. Finally, describe how the door opens: Does it creak open or screech open? Does it rattle or whisper? Does it whine inwards on its hinges?

By the time your protagonist steps through the door, the reader's suspense is turned to high volume, intensely anticipating what happens next.

HEIGHTENING THE SUSPENSE FURTHER

If you want to increase the suspense further still, describe the sound of the door as it closes behind her.

Examples

The door snapped shut.

Behind her, the door groaned shut.

The door thudded closed.

The door clanked into its lock.

This suggests to the reader that the protagonist has just walked into a trap, and that her escape route is blocked.

EXAMPLES FROM BOOKS

Many famous works in literature use the "door effect". Think of Lucy walking through the wardrobe in *The Lion The Witch and The Wardrobe*, or the bride opening the forbidden door in the fairy tale of *Bluebeard*.

Modern masters also use the technique. Here are several examples:

- Alicia Scott (aka Lisa Gardner): *Marrying Mike - Again*

  The huge brass doors loomed ahead of her, the last barrier between her and the press. She could hear the dull roar of news vans and screeching microphones. This was it.

Sandra took a deep breath. She'd run dozens of meetings more important than this; she'd handled situations more critical. She was capable, she was efficient. She would get the job done. And yet her hand was shaking on the large brass handle

[...]

Sandra pushed open the yawning brass doors, and the light bulbs exploded in her face.

- <u>Rebecca Levene: *Cold Warriors*</u>

Raphael raised an eyebrow at him. "In a hurry? Don't worry - we've arrived." He unlocked the steel door in front of him with a rusty key, then swung it open into blackness, stepping aside to beckon Morgan through.

"In there?" Morgan asked dubiously.

Raphael smiled, wrinkling his face into a thousand shallow crevices. "We are very security conscious here - some of our books are worth a great deal of money. After you, Morgan."

It was only when he heard the door slam shut behind him that Morgan remembered he'd never told the professor his name.

- <u>Barbara Nadel: *Belshezzar's Daughter*</u>

He mounted the steps up to the front door. He looked down into the litter-filled well of the basement. Two pairs of rodent eyes stared back at him. He tapped the heavy metal knocker twice and waited.

For at least thirty seconds nothing happened. The rats continued to stare; the silence closed about him like a straitjacket and Robert Cornelius felt the first stirrings of despair, followed quickly by anger.

Then, suddenly and without the usual warning noise of approaching footsteps, the door swung open. "Efendim?"

- <u>Harlan Coben: *Caught*</u>

I knew opening that red door would destroy my life.

Yes, that sounds melodramatic and full of foreboding and I'm not big on either, and true, there was nothing menacing about the red door. In fact, the door was beyond ordinary, wood and fourpaneled, the kind of door you see standing guard in front of three out of every four suburban homes, with faded paint and a knocker at chest level no one ever used and a faux brass knob.

- Angela Carter: *The Lady Of The House Of Love*

  He could almost have regretted accepting the crone's unspoken invitation; but now, standing before the door of time-eroded oak while she selected a huge iron key from the clanking ringful at her waist, he knew it was too late to turn back and brusquely reminded himself he was no child, now, to be frightened of his own fancies.

  The old lady unlocked the door, which swung back on melodramatically creaking hinges, and fussily took charge of his bicycle, in spite of his protests.

  [...]

  But, in for a penny in for a pound - in his youth and strength and blond beauty, in the invisible, even unacknowledged pentacle of his virginity, the young man stepped over the threshold of Nosferatu's castle and did not shiver in the blast of cold air, as from the mouth of a grave that emanated from the lightless, cavernous interior.

- Nicole Young: *Love Me If You Must*

  He walked toward the cellar door.

  "Wait," I hollered when I realized his intentions. "That door stays locked. There's no reason to go down there."

  He paused with his hand on the knob. "Let me do my job, Tish. I want to get some sleep tonight."

  I crossed my arms. "Fine. I'll wait up here."

  "No problem." He turned the latch and stepped into the gloom beyond.

- <u>Karin Slaughter</u>: *Fractured*

  The master key was on his belt. He slid it into the lock and jerked open the door to Warren's cell. The hinge squeaked from the weight of the door.

- <u>Kristine Kathyrn Rusch</u>: *Five Mystery Stories*

  Apartment 14A had a crooked metal sign and an open presswood door, the outside of which had once seen the backside of someone's foot. The breaks in the wood weren't new and they weren't clean, and all they left was a thin layer of really cheap oak covering between the inhabitants - or former inhabitants as the case might be - and the rest of the world.

COLLECTING DOORS

Doors are everywhere, and each door looks, sounds and feels different. Next time you walk through a door, watch and listen. Write your observations down while the memory is fresh. By observing doors wherever you go, you can build a collection of door descriptions for future use. I have almost two hundred doors in my collection, and whenever I need to describe a door, I pick out one that's close to what I want, and adapt it.

Here are some examples from my collection. Bear in mind that these are just notes, not polished writing.

<u>Chinese grocery shop</u>

The dark blue paint was scratched in places, revealing the pale wood underneath. Four glass panels were inserted into the wood. Taped behind them was a Christmas greeting in red glitter-foil, and kitschy Chinese prints of fat happy babies in Santa Claus outfits. The brass door handle squealed when I pressed it down. The door swung inwards without making a noise. When I closed the door behind me, the door handle squealed again, as if in pain.

<u>Private home, middle class, rented, in a small English town</u>

The door was identical to a dozen others in the terrace: mock-Victorian, white-painted wood with arched glass panels at the top, with the house number in gleaming brass. The only thing different was the thick white curtain behind the glass, hiding what might be going on behind. The doorbell gave a soulless 'ping'. I heard shuffling steps, then the rattling of a chain, and the door opened, scraping across the carpet. While I brushed my damp shoes on the door mat - which pictured a fluffy canine with big eyes - the door clacked shut and the chain rattled again.

<u>Youth club for drug addicts in a rough part of town</u>

Black rubbish sacks piled on either side of the narrow wooden door. A laminated sign, nailed to the door, said "Doorbell out of order. Use intercom on the shutter on the right." I glanced to the right, where a hole gaped in the graffiti-smothered wall, suggesting that the intercom as well as the shutter had been ripped out. Below the hole, another sign said 'use other door', with an arrow pointing to the left. I searched, but found no other door, to the left or elsewhere. I checked my appointment diary. This was definitely the address Mrs Nolan had given for our meeting. I returned to the narrow door, and knocked. No response. I banged harder. Young men swaggered past in clusters, yelling at one another. A girl whose black miniskirt barely extended below her crotch stared at me from black-rimmed eyes. Before I could decide whether it was worth asking her for directions, she stalked off on stiletto heels. At last, a light went on behind the smashed glass panel, and the door opened a crack.

DRAWBACKS

You can use this technique several times in a novel, as long as you choose different types of doors, and write each section differently. However, don't be tempted to start every scene in your novel with the protagonist walking through a door: this would be tedious.

The technique works only if something exciting happens once the protagonist has entered. There's no point building suspense by describing how the heroine opens the kitchen door, if all she does is make a cup of tea and then she leaves again. The readers will feel disappointed if you raise their expectations and then don't deliver the promised threat. So make sure there is real danger waiting behind that door.

CHAPTER 4: DARK AND DANGEROUS

Do you want your readers to fear for your heroine's safety? Here's a simple technique on how to make a scene seriously frightening:

Turn the lights off.

Darkness makes people nervous, and everything is much more frightening in the dark. Can you change the time or location of your scene so it happens in darkness? The darker, the better. Absolute darkness is the scariest, when the protagonist sees nothing at all and has to grope to find her way. However, partial darkness can be spooky, too, especially with flickering lights and shadows.

<u>Some ideas for darkness</u>

- A windowless room
- Night time
- Drawn curtains
- A power-cut
- Fuel shortage
- Energy conservation
- Candles burn out
- Wind blows candle
- Lantern falls into abyss
- Bullet shatters light-bulb
- Canopy of trees blocks out the sun
- New moon
- Clouds veil the moon
- Solar eclipse

- Thick smoke

- Sandstorm

- Lights turned off for love-making

- Deep cave

- Hiding in a dark closet

- Flash-light battery dies

- If the storyline permits, let the darkness increase gradually:

- Dusk gives way to night

- The camp-fire burns down

- Clouds thicken

USING THE SENSES

In the dark, humans are deprived of the sense on which they rely most: seeing. Other senses sharpen, especially hearing. Your point-of-view character suddenly hears a lot more noises. These sounds add to the scary effect. In Chapter 5 *Sounds Build Suspense* we'll explore how to make the most of sounds.

If the darkness is absolute, the PoV character relies on her sense of touch as she gropes her way around. Describe how the walls, the furniture, the trees feel to her fingers, and how the ground feels underfoot. Smells also become more noticcable in the dark, and you can give the reader an intense experience by mentioning a smell or two.

Darkness often brings low temperatures. Chills can increase the scare factor, so mention the cool breeze brushing your heroine's arms, the cellar's icy stone walls, the cold water dripping from the ceiling of the cave, the cold seeping through the thin soles of her shoes.

EXAMPLES FROM BOOKS

- Lynda La Plante: *Cold Shoulder*

  It was dark, the alley lit only by neon flashes from the main street; not a single bulb above the many exit doors leading into it remained intact.

- Dean Koontz: <u>*The Bad Place*</u>

  The apartment was a well of shadows, oil-black and pooled deep. Faint ash-gray light outlined the windows but provided no illumination to the room.

- GRR Martin: <u>*Only Kids are Afraid of the Dark*</u>

  No moonlight sifted down; no stars shone from above; only night, sinister and eternal, and the swirling, chocking gray mist that shifted and stirred with every movement.

- Ramsey Campbell: <u>*Heading Home*</u>

  When the flame steadies you can see darkness gaping for inches around the laboratory door.

- Angela Carter: <u>*The Lady of the House of Love*</u>

  Although it was not yet dark outside, the curtains were closely drawn and only the sparing light trickling from a single oil lamp showed him how dismal his surroundings were.

- Tanith Lee: <u>*Wolfland*</u>

  Even with the feeble light, she could barely see ten inches before her, and felt cautiously about with her free hand, dreading to collide with ornament or furniture and thereby rouse her enemies. The stray gleams, shot back at her from a mirror or a picture frame, misled rather than aided her.

DRAWBACKS

This technique suits almost any story, whether you want to send mild shivers across the skin of the paranormal romance reader, or chill the reader's bones in a thriller. However, some scenes need daylight for the plot to work. Also, if scene after scene takes place in the dark, the reader gets so used to it that it's no longer scary.

CHAPTER 5: SOUNDS BUILD SUSPENSE

Of all the senses, the sense of hearing serves best to create excitement, suspense and fear, so use it liberally.

Mention and describe several sounds, and insert those sentences in different sections of the scene. This technique suits all stories in all genres. It works especially well if the scene is set in darkness, because the sense of hearing is sharpened when the vision is reduced.

ACTION SOUNDS

Use the sounds of the ongoing action, especially of the threat: the villain's footsteps clanking down the metal stairs, the dungeon door squealing open, the rasp of the prison guard's voice, the attack dog's growl, the rattling of the torture instruments in the tool box.

BACKGROUND SOUNDS

In addition, use the background noises which aren't connected to the action. Think about the noises of the setting.

<u>Examples</u>

A shutter banged against the frame.

A car door slammed. A motor whined.

A dog howled in the distance.

The motor stuttered and whined.

The ceiling fan whirred.

The wind whined.

The rope clanked rhythmically against the flagpole.

Computers beeped, phones shrilled, and printers whirred.

Waves hissed against the shore.

Waves thumped against the hull.

Thunder rumbled.

Rodent feet scurried.

Water gurgled in the drainpipe.

EXTREME SUSPENSE

A few 'sound' sentences work wonders for the atmosphere of your scary scene. You can insert them wherever it makes sense - and even in random places.

The most powerful use of this technique is to make a suspenseful moment even more suspenseful.

By inserting a sentence about an irrelevant background noise, you can slow the pace without lowering the excitement. This turns the tension and suspense up several notches.

Here's an example:

Before

The knife came closer to her throat. And closer.

She squirmed against the bonds, knowing it to be useless.

The cold edge of steel touched her skin. She tried not to swallow.

After

The knife came closer to her throat. And closer.

She squirmed against the bonds, knowing it to be useless.

Somewhere in the distance, a car door slammed and a motor whined.

The cold edge of steel touched her skin. She tried not to swallow.

COLLECTING SOUNDS

Whenever you're away from home and have a few moments to spare, listen to the noises around you. Jot them down in your writer's notebook. (If you don't have a writer's notebook yet, get one: a small lightweight one with ruled pages is practical.)

If possible, describe what the noises sound like, using verbs (*a car rattles up the road* or a car *whines up the road*)

By observing and noting the noises of one place per day (365 places per year), you can build a fantastic resource which will come in handy for future fiction projects. This is also a handy way of killing time, especially in boring meetings, at the laundrette, at the railway station, in a queue, and in the dentist's waiting room. Use the time constructively for writing research.

You can even swap noise notes with other writers. Your writing buddy may be working on a scene set in an abandoned mine-shaft - and you may have notes about the sounds in such a place. Or you may write a scene set in the Brazilian jungle - where she took notes during her trip last year.

CHAPTER 6: TOTAL ISOLATION

Solitary adventures are more dangerous than group adventures. In nature, an animal which becomes separated from the herd is vulnerable to predators. To make your scene scary, let your heroine face the danger alone.

The more you isolate your protagonist, the more frightening the scene becomes. Think of as many ways as possible to make her even more cut off from rescue and moral support.

SEND THE ALLIES AWAY

Give your protagonist a reason why she faces this danger on her own.

Perhaps she has no choice: the little girl is alone in the house because her parents have gone to the theatre. The hero's guide and friends have been killed leaving him as the only survivor. The explorer's companions have stolen his equipment and deserted him. The prisoner escaped from the dungeon and is fleeing alone.

On the other hand, she may have chosen to do this alone: the treasure hunter doesn't want to share the bounty with others. The teenager quarrelled with her date and told him to leave her alone. The explorer is the only one who believes that the coded map reveals the true location of the temple; when others mocked his belief he set out on his own.

Sometimes, when the adventure stretches over several scenes, you can take away the protagonist's companions one by one. First, his friends declare him crazy and refuse to join the expedition, so he sets out with his girlfriend, three mates, and a local guide. Then his girlfriend falls in love with one of his mates, and the two depart. The local guide steals the equipment and deserts. One of his loyal companions gets killed by a giant snake, the second by the evil overlord's poisoned arrow. Now he's alone.

In other works of fiction, the protagonist may be alone for only part of the scene. For example, the hero and heroine are exploring the castle ruins together. Then the hero gets captured by the villains, or maybe he leaves the group to fetch supplies from the car or to investigate a mysterious signal, and the heroine faces the danger alone. For the last part of the scene, they're together again, but the danger is not yet over.

CUT THE LINES OF COMMUNICATION

To isolate your protagonist even more, deprive her of the means of calling for help. The villains have cut the telephone lines. A blizzard prevents other people from coming to this place. The radio battery is empty so the explorer can no longer send Morse signals. The computer has crashed. The internet server is down.

For the writer of scary scenes, mobile phones (American: "cell phones") are a nuisance. The scene isn't really scary if your heroine can summon help at any time. Make sure she doesn't have a mobile phone with her, or that it isn't functioning: Her bag was stolen, or she lost it during her daring escape or had to drop it while running for her life. She doesn't own a mobile phone because she hates modern technology. There is no reception in the remote mountain valley. She forgot to recharge the battery. She couldn't afford to pay for a top-up. She borrowed a friend's mobile phone and the friend forgot to tell her that the service has been disconnected.

NOBODY KNOWS

There must be no chance of a lucky rescue, either. Nobody must miss her, or even know where she is. The treasure hunter laid a false trail about his destination. The teenager didn't tell her parents where she was going because she knew they wouldn't approve. The police officer did not tell her colleagues because what she plans on doing is not strictly legal. The heroine tells no one where she's going because she doesn't want her stalking ex-boyfriend to find her. The hiker told the landlord of the last inn that he planned to walk south, but then changed his mind and went west.

PROFESSIONAL EXAMPLES

Copyright rules prevent me from quoting excerpts longer than a few lines, so I can't show you examples of how professional writers use this technique. However, you'll find that many bestselling authors use it in their fiction. Among Victorian writers, Amelia Edwards excelled at it. Among modern horror writers, Stephen King has used this technique in many of his stories.

DRAWBACKS

This technique does not work for every story. Some plots require that two or more people face the danger together. You may be able to compromise, for example, the heroine and hero stay together, but they lose their mobile phone and are unable to summon help.

CHAPTER 7: STRIP TO TEASE

Here's a nifty psychological trick to torment the reader's subconscious with suspense: tell your protagonist to strip off her clothes.

VULNERABILITY

Clothing is protective armour. By undressing, the protagonist is giving up that last layer of protection.

Some stories allow total nudity: The honeymoon bride expects her new husband to come into the bedroom. The life model is posing for an artist. The girl steps into the shower.

For most stories, the protagonist takes off only one layer of clothing: On entering the well-heated cottage, the visitor takes off his coat, hat and gloves. The heroine tears her skirt into strips to use as bandaging for the wounded hero. The prisoner knots his garments together to use as a rope by which he lowers himself from the window. The young woman takes off her cumbersome long narrow skirt to run faster. The bather takes off all but his swimming trunks to go for a swim. The fighter takes off his tight jacket to have more freedom of movement. The bride strips down to her sexy lingerie for her wedding night. Having splashed tomato sauce on her designer blouse, she takes it off to rinse it under the tap before the stain becomes permanent. The teen takes off her cardigan because none of the other girls is wearing one. She takes off her jacket because she wants to let her date see her sparkly halter-neck. She rips off the scarf because it was a gift from the boyfriend and she has just found out that he's been cheating on her. She slips off her sandals because she likes to feel the hot sand under her soles. The driver of the broken-down car removes his jacket because he doesn't want it to get dirty while he fixes the motor.

SLOW TEASE

If the plot permits, you can increase the suspense by removing one garment after the other, slowly and deliberately, like a striptease artiste.

<u>Examples</u>

He slipped out of his jacket and hung it over the car seat, so it would not crease. Then loosened his shirt collar and rolled up his sleeves.

She slipped out of her high-heeled shoes and tossed them into the corner. One stocking followed, then the other. She unzipped her gown and pulled it over her head.

This "slow striptease" technique is especially effective if the reader already suspects danger, but the protagonist is still unaware.

DRAWBACKS

If used several times in a novel, especially the full striptease, the reader will notice the repetition. It can become ridiculous.

CHAPTER 8: KEEP THE CLOCK TICKING

To add excitement and suspense to your scene, consider using the "ticking clock" technique.

You have already established a scene goal for your protagonist. If he must achieve this goal in a certain time, and if missing the deadline will bring dire consequences, then the reader will watch the clock. The more time passes, the higher the tension.

TYPES OF CLOCK

Sometimes, the ticking clock is real: a grandfather clock which goes tock-tock-tock, a clock on the steeple of a German village church, an expensive Rolex watch with silver hands, a children's alarm-clock with a Winnie-the-Pooh face, or an egg-timer with purple sand.

The passing time can also be measured in other ways:

- The weather (she needs to finish a task before the rain starts)
- Rhythms of nature (she needs to get to the shore before the incoming tide reaches her, or she needs to get out of the castle before night falls and the vampires waken)
- The actions of other people (she needs to reach the place before her rival does)
- Progressing disaster (he needs to get across the bridge before it collapses completely).

HOW TO USE THE TICKING CLOCK

At the beginning of the scene, establish how much time the protagonist has to achieve his goal, or to accomplish something else. Emphasise the dire consequences should he fail to do it by that time (the vampires will get him, the bomb will explode, the hostages will be executed). Alternatively, mention that a certain terrible thing will happen at a certain time.

Then, throughout the scene, show several times how time is passing: the hands of the clock shifting, the sand running through the spout, the sun sinking towards the horizon.

Example of a "ticking clock"

Dan checked his watch: 2.50. He had fifteen minutes to save his daughter.

Fifteen minutes to find the right house in this blasted street in blasted semi-suburbia, to break down the door, to fight her abductors, to free her from captivity, to get her to safety.

Each house in this street was the same: red brick, sash windows, white doors. No movement, nothing out of place. Not a single net curtain twitched.

Two dozen terraced homes, created by an unimaginative architect and a cost-saving builder, lived-in by labourers who craved middle-class respectability. Behind one of these pristine doors, Sharleen awaited execution.

They would kill her at 3.05.

The blue hand of Dan's watch said 2.54.

Which door? Holy Hades, which?

The one with the cute-puppy doormat? Or the flowered enamel number plate? The twinkling fairy lights, or the fat plastic Santa?

Why, oh why, hadn't he pressed his daughter for details before she left the house? 2.57. Eight minutes left.

Even the front gardens were the same, square patches of lawn, each with a winter-bare rose bush in the centre.

He would smash his way into those fake respectable doors, splinter the wood, rip the hangings. But while he barged through one home, Sharleen would die in another. He had to get it right.

From number fourteen, a man emerged. Dark jacket, dog on a leash.

"Excuse me, Sir." Dan fought to keep his voice calm, even as his heart was thumping. "I wonder if you can help me. I'm looking for a girl. Fourteen, blonde. Wearing a school uniform -"

"Can't help you," the man said coldly, giving Dan a look which said 'Paedophile!' and tugged at the leash. "Come, Buster."

"Sir, it's not what you think..."

The man didn't turn.

The church clock chimed. High, sharp rings: one, two, three.

In five minutes, Sharleen would be dead.

CLIMAX IN THE LAST POSSIBLE MOMENT

To make the most of the 'ticking clock', let your protagonist achieve his goal in the final minute - or even the final second. This creates a tense, suspenseful scene climax which has the readers biting their nails.

Once the goal is achieved, the exhausted hero may hear or see the clock reaching the fatal mark, emphasising how narrowly he has won.

DRAWBACKS

This technique doesn't work for every scene. Sometimes, the ticking clock can be applied only to part of the scene, or not at all.

If several scenes have ticking clocks, they need to be different types of clock, or it becomes boring.

If the overall plot of the novel has a ticking clock (for example, the hero in the thriller has two weeks to save the world), then additional ticking clocks for individual scenes (he has one hour to raise the cash, and thirty minutes to decipher the code) can be distracting.

CHAPTER 9: FEEL THE FEAR

To make the reader feel the protagonist's fear, show us the physical effects of being frightened.

SHOW DON'T TELL

Telling the reader about the hero's fear is useless. You need to show it. "Showing" is probably not visual, but visceral: a sensation of the body.

"Telling" examples

- He felt frightened.
- She was scared.
- I grew very afraid.
- He experienced a really terrible emotion of utter fear, a feeling that was indescribably scary.

"Showing" examples

- Fear prickled her scalp.
- Her breath stalled.
- Fear clenched like a tight first around my chest.
- Tendrils of terror curled into her stomach.
- Cold sweat trickled down her sides.
- His heart thudded louder and louder.
- Fear clogged his throat.
- My pulse pounded in my throat.
- Cold sweat glued the shirt to his back.
- Chills chased up my back.

- Common sense warned me to stay in my hiding place, but I needed a toilet. Now.

- The sight made the back of my neck tingle.

- I could hear the blood rushing through my head.

- My skull seemed to shrink.

- A ball of fear formed in my stomach.

- My stomach knotted.

- My stomach swelled with fear.

- A weight seemed to press on her chest, robbing her of breath.

- A thousand ants seemed to crawl over my skin.

PHYSICAL SYMPTOMS

When a human is frightened, lots of things happen to the body.

The person may feel hot or cold, may shiver or sweat.

The heart beats faster, harder, louder. The person may hear or feel their own heart beat in unusual places: in their ears, in their throat.

The breathing changes. Usually it becomes faster and shallower, though for some people it may deepen and slow.

The palms may become damp, the mouth dry, the stomach tight, the throat clogged.

Fear can make a person yawn, though you need to be careful with this so you don't accidentally suggest boredom.

The skin reacts. There may be goose-pimples ('goosebumps' in American). The little hairs may stand up in some places. Often, there's an itch, most commonly on the head, though it can occur anywhere, and this itch may be very inconvenient when someone tries hard not to move.

The stomach may clench, or churn, or feel like it's filled with ice.

Smokers may desperately crave a cigarette.

Some people feel fear in strange places, e.g. the fillings of their teeth hurt.

During prolonged apprehension, pressure on the bladder builds, resulting in an urge to use the loo ('bathroom' in American). In moments of panic, the bladder may open, and in a state of terror, the bowels may loosen.

Simply insert a sentence about a physical symptom, and the reader's heart will accelerate with the hero's, and shivers will crawl over their skin just like the heroine's.

AVOID CLICHÉS

If possible, avoid the clichéd phrases, or rephrase them in a fresh way.

Instead of the clichéd "A shiver ran down her spine" you could write:

A shiver slid down the length of her spine.

or:

Shivers crawled up her spine.

When describing how the heart beats, consider replacing the word "beat" with a more evocative verb:

- His heart thudded.
- His heart pounded.
- His heart hammered.
- His heart raced.

Instead of "heart" you can sometimes use "pulse":

- His pulse raced.
- His pulse thudded in his ears.

VARY THE INTENSITY

You can insert several 'physical symptom' sentences into a scary scene. You may want to vary the symptoms, e.g. when she first feels foreboding, her scalp tingles. When she realises there is danger, her stomach tightens and her palms grow wet. When the villain involves her in conversation, her throat is so dry she can't get a word out. When she's tied up and she hears the bomb ticking, her stomach contorts, cold sweat soaks her clothes, and her heart thuds as if it were trying to break out of her ribcage.

At the scariest moment, you can cluster two or three visceral effects closely together.

DRAWBACKS

Although you can use physical symptoms of fear several times in each scary scene, take care not to use them much elsewhere in your novel. If the hero's heart starts pounding every time a door bangs, and if sweat trickles down his spine every time he faces a challenge, he'll come across as a wimp.

Choose symptoms appropriate to the situation, the character, the desired scariness-level, and the genre - and don't overdo it. Opening bladders and loosening bowels are fine for the climax of an ultra-scary thriller or horror novel - but in a Regency romance they're out of place.

CHAPTER 10: PACING

In a scary scene, the pace may vary from extremely slow to ultra-fast, so you need to use techniques for speeding and slowing the pace.

FAST PACE

When the action happens fast - for instance, during a fist fight, or when the heroine runs for her life - your writing style needs to reflect the speed of the action.

<u>Writing techniques for fast pace</u>

- No description.

- No extraneous detail.

- Few, if any, adjectives and adverbs.

- Short paragraphs, short sentences, short words.

Short sentences are especially useful, because their rhythm conveys breathlessness and a racing heart. By speeding up the pace, you can increase the excitement.

Cut out every superfluous word. Split long and medium-length sentences into several short ones. You can even use partial sentences. Yes, even if you normally write in full, grammatically correct sentences. Moments of danger justify the broken sentences. The staccato effect creates a sense of racing pace. Of danger. Of fear.

Here are some examples how sentences can be shortened, tightened and split to convey that sense of hurry and danger:

Before

She could feel her stomach tightening and her heart beating faster. Deciding that she must get away, she took the box from the table and started to run towards what she hoped would be safety.

After

Her heart hammered. Her stomach clenched. She snatched the box and ran.

Before

She scanned the room, searching for a weapon, but found nothing.

After

She scanned the room for a weapon. Nothing.

Before

She shook him by the shoulders, but received no response. When she checked his eyes, she observed that they were glassy and still, and concluded that he was dead.

After

She shook his shoulders. No response. His eyes were glassy, still. Dead.

Before

He realised that he could feel his skin crawling with a strange sensation.

After

His skin crawled.

Before

He considered waiting longer, but eventually decided to jump immediately because the moment was right.

After

Now. He jumped.

Before

In the meantime, someone seemed to be walking, apparently wearing boots which made a hard sound on the floor.

After

Boots clanked.

SLOW PACE

The parts of your scene where your protagonist is waiting, desperately hoping for something to happen - or not to happen - and unable to do anything, benefit from a slower pace. Indeed, by slowing the pace you can increase the suspense.

Writing techniques for slow pace
- Medium-length to long paragraphs
- Medium-length to long sentences
- Words of varying length
- Some adjectives, maybe a few adverbs
- Using several senses (seeing, hearing, smelling, touching, tasting, temperature, pain etc).
- Descriptions

The descriptions are the most useful slow-pace technique in scary scenes, because they allow you to create a spooky atmosphere.

Describing background noises is highly effective for slowing the pace and building suspense.

DRAWBACKS

The pace of the writing needs to reflect the pace of the action, and in a scary scene, it needs to vary.

The effect of ultra-fast paced writing wears off after a few paragraphs, so use it only for the very fast moments, especially the clipped sentences.

Slow-paced writing, if it goes on for too long, bores the reader who may start skipping. Use it only for a few paragraphs, and don't overdo the long sentences and the adverbs.

CHAPTER 11: EUPHONICS

This technique is a subtle trick for manipulating the reader's subconscious.

Certain sounds have certain effects on the psyche. By using words which include those sounds, you influence how the reader feels.

SCARY-SOUNDING WORDS

These are the sound effects you can use for scary scenes:

Foreboding

Use words with OW, OH, OU, OO sounds: *howl, moor, growl, slow, wound, soon, doom.* These are perfect for those prolonged moments of suspense, when the hero isn't yet in danger, but the reader already senses that something is very wrong. The heroine entering the forbidden garden, or the hero waiting outside the door waiting for it to open, are good places for this kind of euphonic technique.

Spooky

Use words with S sounds, if possible combined with short I sounds *(hiss, sizzle, crisp, sister, whisper, sinister)*. These are especially good for ghost stories.

Acute fear

Use words with EE/EA sounds, if possible combine with a few S sounds *(squeal, scream, stream, squeeze, creak, steal, sheer)*. This is perfect to use when the protagonist is aware of the danger and feels scared.

Fights and action

Use words, especially short verbs, with T, P and K sounds: *(cut, block, top, shoot, tackle, trick, kick)*. Use this for the section where the heroine fights to free herself from the villain's clutches, or defends herself against the werewolf attack.

Speed, running

Use short words which contain R: *run, race, riot, roll, rip, hurry, scurry, ring*. This works great for moments when the protagonist runs for her life.

Plot complications, anticipating problems

Use words which contain TR: *trouble, trap, trip, trough, treat, trick, treasure, atrocious, attract, petrol, trance, try, traitor*. These serve well when the protagonist realises he's in trouble. Consider combining this with the "foreboding" sounds.

REPLACE WORDS

When revising a draft, it's easy to replace some words with substitutes which contain the right sound.

For example, if you want to convey acute fear, instead of "food" you could write "meal", instead of "wine" you could write "beer", instead of "butter" you could write "cream". If you want spookiness, instead of 'his brother muttered' you could write 'his sibling whispered'. If you want foreboding, instead of 'the spaniel barked', write 'the hound growled'.

While *the storm howled up the road* is good for foreboding, *the wind whistled between the houses* is good for spookiness.

In a ghost story, Sibyl sips her drink, slips into her silky camisole, and listens as the wind whispers and the water tap drips.

Earlier, we explored the techniques of making the protagonist pass through a doorway, and of using sounds to create scariness. You can combine these two techniques with euphonics. Here are some examples, showing the subtle difference:

Foreboding

The door groaned open.

The door moaned shut.

Spooky

The door hissed open.

The door whispered shut.

Frightening

The door creaked open.

The door squealed shut.

PERFORMANCE

Euphonics are especially powerful when the reader actually hears the words. If you're writing a story for radio, are planning to publish your novel as an audiobook, or intend to give author readings at your local book shop, euphonics help enthral your audience.

DRAWBACKS

In print, the effects of this technique are very subtle, serving only to enhance what's already there. It needs to be combined with other techniques.

If you use too many similar-sounding words close together, the effect can be comical rather than scary.

Using words which have the right sound but the wrong meaning weakens your scene. Use euphonics only when there's a choice of suitable words.

CHAPTER 12: PEAKS AND TROUGHS

Constant terror soon gets dull. The readers can't sustain continuous scared excitement, and after a while, instead of roused, they become bored.

It's like the waves on a stormy sea: the peaks are only high because of the troughs between them. If there were only continuous peaks without any troughs, the sea would be flat.

Your job as writer is to create not just the peaks, but the troughs which make the peaks look high.

Allow your protagonist to relax and get her breath back before throwing her into the next scary experience. During this brief relaxation of the tension, your reader's heartbeat returns to normal - so it can accelerate again.

Here's what the scary part of your story might look like if it consisted only of peaks, and how a skilled writer might handle it by alternating peaks and troughs.

Peaks-only version
- The heroine gets tortured by the villain. (peak)
- She escapes by scaling the dungeon walls. (peak)
- As soon as she's outside, she gets pursued by a charging bull. (peak)
- To get away from the bull, she crawls into a narrow cave where she is immediately attacked by a snake. (peak)

This is too much relentless scare. By the time the heroine faces the snake, the reader scarcely cares anymore.

<u>Peaks & troughs version</u>

- The heroine gets tortured by the villain. (peak)
- Finally, he retires for the night, and the pain ceases. (trough)
- She escapes by scaling the dungeon walls. (peak)
- Outside, there's bright light, clean air, the scents of meadow flowers. (trough)
- A bull comes charging. (peak)
- To escape from the bull, she crawls into a narrow cave. The bull can't get in. She catches her breath and bandages her wounds and lies down to get some much-needed sleep. (trough)
- A hiss alerts her to the presence of a dangerous snake. (peak)

The troughs don't have to be long. One paragraph is often enough. You can insert a short trough in the middle of a scary scene, or as a transition between two scary scenes. At other times, you may want to insert a whole "trough" scene between two "peak" scenes. For example, in the climax of a thriller, you can insert a non-scary scene, perhaps a tender love scene, between two terrifying sections.

DRAWBACKS

If the troughs are too long, or if there are many of them, they can make your writing boring. Don't allow your reader to become too relaxed. Use the troughs sparingly and keep them short.

CHAPTER 13: STRUCTURING A SCARY SCENE

There's no standard structure you must follow. However, here's a structure which suits many major scary scenes. You can use it as a blueprint for your own scene, or simply as a starting point. Feel free to adapt it, to add to it or to leave bits out. Make it work for you.

PART 1: SCENE GOAL

Tell the reader what the protagonist needs to achieve, and why. State the goal clearly, and remind the reader what's at stake. This can be part of a dialogue, or simply a statement. See Chapter 2 *Instant Hooks*. Make it bold and clear. This section is very short, usually just one paragraph. The character's main emotions are anxiety and suspense, possibly blended with apprehension or dread.

PART 2: SUSPENSE

The protagonist knowingly enters a dangerous situation. Often, the protagonist passes through some kind of barrier – climbing across a fence, entering through a door, ducking under a rope, crawling into a cave mouth. This section is often several paragraphs long. Use vivid descriptions, especially of sounds. See Chapter 5 *Sounds Build Suspense*. The protagonist feels apprehension, foreboding or dread. The reader feels suspense.

PART 3: INCREASED DANGER

The danger turns out to be greater than the hero bargained for. The allies and tools on which he relied let him down. In this section, his friends desert him, his torch fails, the weapon drops into the abyss and the mobile phone battery runs out. In this section, the protagonist feels apprehension or dread, possibly punctuated with other emotions such as anger and frustration. The reader feels suspense. Make sure that the protagonist does something during this section (scale a wall, dig a tunnel, break a safe); there needs to be action, not just emotion.

PART 4: FIRST CONFRONTATION

The hero comes face to face with one of the villain's henchmen (it can be a bodyguard, a ferocious guard dog, a robot, a police officer or an unruffled secretary) and needs to outwit or defeat them. This section often involves physical fighting. Use hard-sounding euphonics in this section, and vary the sentence length. During the fighting, the sentences can be very short. Aim for excitement, perhaps mixed with apprehension, revulsion or horror.

PART 5: ESCAPE

The hero manages a narrow escape. Either he succeeds in defeating his opponent, or he runs for his life. See Chapter 19 *Chases and Escapes.* The pace in this section is very fast. Use short paragraphs, sentences and short words.

PART 6: TROUGH

After the Escape section, there is often a brief trough when the hero thinks he's safe. See Chapter12 *Peaks and Troughs.* The tension slackens for a moment, giving the reader a chance to breathe. The pace slows, so use longer sentences. Keep this section very short – probably just one paragraph. Don't let your reader relax for too long.

PART 7: REALISATION

The protagonist realises that he has made a mistake. Perhaps he comprehends that the opponent he defeated a moment ago was not the villain himself but a mere henchman. Or maybe he sees that he has walked into a trap. The fear in this situation is intense. He may feel a moment's panic – and in his panic, make another mistake. Vary the sentence lengths.

PART 8: MAIN CONFRONTATION

The hero meets the villain. See Chapter 17 *Villains and Monsters*. There may be a fight. The villain has many advantages on his side: he expected the hero, he fights on home ground, he is strong and well-equipped. The pace is fast, so use short sentences. The fear is intense, but the protagonist needs to be in control of his emotions in order to take action, so avoid terror and panic. This section should be longer than the others: allow several paragraphs.

PART 9: AFTERMATH

The hero has either escaped or is imprisoned (see Chapter 18 *Captivity*) and doomed. Either way, he is no longer in acute danger. Write this section as a "trough" and slow the pace with longer sentences. The protagonist probably assesses his situation and forms a plan. End the section with the hero's resolution to take specific action.

CHAPTER 14: CHOOSING THE LOCATION

Set your scene in the right location, and it will be frightening and memorable.

DARK

If possible, choose a venue which is dark, either pitch-black or shadow-haunted. This will allow you to use the techniques from Chapter 4 *Dark and Dangerous.*

Here are some ideas for dark locations
- Outdoors, at dusk
- Outdoors, at night
- Outdoors, storm clouds blocking the sun
- Garden shed without light
- Unlit or sparsely lit cellar
- Unlit attic
- Abandoned mine shaft
- Ruined building
- Modern building during a powercut
- Forest with dense tree canopy
- Cave
- Trapped by a mudslide or avalanche
- Catacombs
- Unlit mausoleum or crypt

COLD

It also helps if the place has an unpleasant temperature, especially if it's cold. Apply the techniques from Chapter 15 *Using the Senses.*

Ideas for cold locations

- Food storage cellar
- Wine cellar
- Dungeon
- Skiing piste
- Night outdoors
- Nightfall, trapped in cable car
- Old mine shaft
- Unheated building
- Ruined building
- Outdoors, weather turning cold
- Indoors, heater failure or power cut
- Mausoleum or crypt
- Cave
- Mountain hut
- Buried under an avalanche

SPOOKY

Certain locations evoke fear in the reader even if no threat is present. You can use these associations to plant fear into the reader's subconscious. This works especially well with places considered spooky.

Ideas for spooky locations

- Cemetery, graveyard
- Haunted house
- Old castle

- Ruined building
- Dungeon
- Execution site
- Catacomb
- Crypt, mausoleum
- Building formerly used as prison

UNFAMILIAR

If the PoV doesn't know the place, if everything is strange and alien, if she has no idea where the exit lies or the high tide comes, this creates natural anxiety for the protagonist as well as for the reader. This "fish out of the water" technique has been used by storytellers and writers in all cultures, from fairy tales to thrillers, from Victorian gothic novels to 20th century romantic suspense. It is one of the easiest techniques, and hugely effective. Try it.

FAMILIAR

On the other hand, if you want to unsettle the reader on a deep level, choose a location where the character feels safe – the kind of place where neither the character nor the reader expects danger. Familiar places, and sites of harmless activities are especially effective. This breaches psychological boundaries makes the scene all the more frightening. Scary scenes set in seemingly harmless locations stay in the reader's mind.

Ideas for locations perceived as safe

- Bedroom
- Kitchen
- Playground
- Kindergarten

- Church or other place of worship of the PoV's own faith
- Gym (the one the character attends regularly)

ISOLATED

If the character is alone in the place, with no one to help him and no way to call for help, the scare factor will multiply. Choose a location where the character is isolated from the outside world. You may want to use the suggestions from Chapter 7 *Strip to Tease* to increase the isolation and make sure nobody even knows where the character has gone.

Ideas for isolated locations

- Cave
- Abandoned mine shaft
- Ruined building
- Wreck underwater
- Cable car
- Mountaintop
- Mountain cabin
- Disused property
- Wasteland
- Locked prison cell
- Railway tunnel

DANGEROUS

Some locations are dangerous. If the hero faces the menacing villain in a place where he can't simply run away, he has to choose between two dangers. This is guaranteed to get your reader's heart racing.

Ideas for dangerous locations
- Cliff top
- Under water
- Mine shaft
- Near explosives
- In a building about to collapse/burn/explode
- Top of a skyscraper building
- Narrow/wobbly/crumbling bridge across an abyss
- Mudslide
- Snake pit
- Jungle
- Nature reserve with wild lions or leopards
- Zoo cage
- Boat on shark-infested water
- Laboratory with acid substances
- Rollercoaster

TRAPPED

If your character is trapped in a place where he can't get out, everything becomes intense, including the fear. For some readers, this can raise the fear to almost unbearable levels.

Ideas for trap locations
- Cable car dangling over abyss
- Rope bridge with villains waiting either end
- Mine shaft
- Cave
- Zoo cage
- Prison cell

- Dungeon
- Collapsed building
- Avalanche
- Crypt
- Coffin

Whatever location you choose, use it to the full. Make it dark and cold if you can, insert many noises (see Chapter 5 *Sounds Build Suspense)* and show how the textures feel to the character's probing touch.

CHAPTER 15: USING THE SENSES

By describing the PoV's experiences with sensory detail, you pull the reader deep into the experience. For best effect, use at least three different senses in your scene.

How many senses are there? Aristotle 384 BC – 322 BC identified five: seeing, hearing, touching, smelling, tasting.

Other scientists have identified additional senses, for instance, pain, balance, temperature and psychic awareness.

To writers, the number and definition of senses matters little. What counts is that you use several senses, and use them often.

Here are the senses most relevant to scary scenes.

SEEING

This sense is most writers first choice, because it's the easiest. But it's also the least powerful, and when it comes to scaring readers, it doesn't help much. Try to use it sparingly in your scary scenes. The less you rely on it, the more intense the reader's experience becomes.

Be selective about what you describe visually. Good uses are the effects of darkness and moving shadows, the villain's eyes, the monster's claws.

If you are revising a draft, consider the visual descriptions you've used, and see if you can replace some of them with sounds or smells. This will make your scene more vivid and intense. The difference from changing a few sentences can be awesome.

HEARING

If you want to excite or scare your readers, this is the sense to use. Whenever you describe something – a person, an object, a place – ask yourself "What noise does this make?" and describe the sounds. This includes the villain's voice, the squeaking step, the squeal of car tyres, and the banging of a door. A single sentence about a sound creates more atmosphere than several sentences of visual description. Sounds also create excitement and, unlike other descriptions, don't bog down the pace.

Best of all, sounds intensify every flavour of fear, especially suspense, terror and dread.

During moments of suspenseful waiting, mention background sounds.

For specific ideas on how to use sounds, see Chapter 5 *Sounds Build Suspense.*

SMELLING

The sense of smell is the writer's most powerful tool. A single sentence about smells creates a more intense experience for the reader than a page of visual descriptions. Whenever your PoV arrives at a new place or meets a new person, describe the smell.

The room smelled of urine and disinfectant.

He smelled of beer and sweat.

The sense of smell is especially strong when the air is warm, and when the sense of seeing is reduced because of darkness.

Use smells whenever you want to create revulsion, in scenes of captivity (what does the place smell of?), to hint at a person's character and background (does the man threatening the heroine smell of cigarettes and motor oil and sweat, or of mint mouthwash and Italian aftershave?)

In horror and thrillers, you can use all kinds of smells, but in romance and erotica, smells should be mostly pleasant so as not to spoil the reader's pleasure.

TOUCHING

If your PoV is in a situation of danger, or if it is dark, the sense of touching is perfect. Describe what the ground feels like underfoot (hard, soft, squishy, spongy, slippery, bumpy) and what she feels with her hands, especially if she has to grope her way in the darkness. Does she touch cool smooth tile, rough stone, smooth stone, slippery, slimy? Whenever your PoV feels something through touch which she does not see, this creates fear in the reader, often apprehension, revulsion or terror.

When she gropes her way along the walls, or crawls down the narrow tunnel, is the surface she touches rough, smooth, warm, cold, damp, hard, soft, slippery, slimy?

You can also describe things touching her, the rain stinging her cheeks, her captor's grip on her arm, the cobwebs in her face, the sharp stones stabbing into her flesh when she tries to sleep on the ground, the spider tickling up her leg.

TASTING

Not every scene needs the sense of taste. You can skip this, unless your heroine is having dinner with the villain, or sipping water in her prison cell. However, if she's been in a fight, she may taste blood (metallic). She could also have a sour taste in her mouth as a reaction to something she learns, or she might taste bile.

BALANCE

Use this sense only if your character's sense of balance is disturbed, for example, if she is dizzy from rolling down a slope, disoriented from shock, or woozy from staring at the 3,000-foot drop below her. There may be a painful lightness in her head, nausea in her stomach, her breathing becomes shallow, she clings to anything she can grab hold of. Her steps become unsteady. You would not use this sense often, but once in a book is effective.

TEMPERATURE

This is a good sense to use in scary scenes. What's the temperature of the place like? If possible, make it either hot or cold, not pleasantly temperate. The temperature can increase either her shivers or her sweat.

What is she wearing? It helps if she is dressed inappropriately for the weather or the location. Let her sweat in her thick jumper or shiver in her flimsy dress. This works well in connection with the technique from Chapter 7 *Strip To Tease*.

Mention the temperature of the air, and also of anything she touches with her hands, as well as what touches her skin. Describe the chill seeping from the concrete floor through her sandal soles, the icy wind lashing her cheeks, the cold rain creeping into her clothes, the hot blast from the furnace making it difficult to breathe, or the sun searing her bare skin.

PSYCHIC AWARENESS

Important in fantasy and paranormal romance, but also in other genres. It manifests itself in physical sensations. The person may feel a sudden chill, a heaviness in the stomach, a crawling of the skin, or may hear a ringing in the head, or a faint hum in the air. There may be an aura-like light surrounding a person or object, or it could be an envelope of darkness. Visions may flash in the character's head, or she may hear voices.

These symptoms vary from person to person. Your character will experience only one or two of them.

If she is an experienced psychic, perhaps trained in psychic reading, she will know what these sensations mean, and interpret them correctly. On the other hand, if she does not have the knowledge or training, she may simply shiver and not know why.

The sense of psychic awareness works best in situations of unease or foreboding.

PAIN

The sense of pain plays a role in many scary scenes: Groping her way through a light-less corridor, the heroine bangs her head against something. Chains or fetters chafe her ankles. The villain slams his fist into her back. Fleeing for her life, she stumbles and sprains her ankle.

Describe the pain: Is it piercing, thudding, burning, searing, pulsing, sharp or dull?

Think about when your protagonist feels the hurt. Most pain happens at once. But during a fight or race for safety, adrenaline often dulls the pain. She may not even realise she's been hurt until the danger is over, the adrenaline wears off, and the pain kicks in.

If she's had a shock, time may pass before she feels the pain from her wounds.

CHAPTER 16: CLIFFHANGERS

To keep the reader going, turning page after page even when she meant to do the dishes or go to sleep, place an exciting hook at the end of every scene.

Don't end a scene with everything resolved, good and well. Instead, make the reader tense about what happens next.

SCENE-ENDING HOOKS

In Chapter 2 *Instant Hooks* you chose a scene goal. By stating this goal at the beginning of the scene, you placed the reader in suspense about "Will the PoV achieve the goal?"

The end of the scene should answer this question – but preferably not with a straight "yes" because that would end the tension. The reader, her curiosity satisfied, would put the book away and wash the dishes.

A much better scene ending is "Yes, the PoV achieves the goal, but... a new complication has arisen, and she must deal with it." Another good one is "She achieved only part of her goal, and to get the rest, she has to do something dangerous." Sometimes you can even end a scene like this: "No, she did not achieve her goal, and her situation has become worse than before."

POV IN PERIL

A scene which ends where the PoV is in acute trouble with no obvious way out (such as dangling from a cliff top, about to fall as soon as her arms' strength gives out) is called a "cliffhanger" and it's a sure way to make the reader turn to the next page. Even if she decides to take a break and do the dishes, she'll return to the book soon because she simply must find out how the PoV gets out of this.

This technique works superbly with scary scenes. Put your PoV in a dangerous situation – if not dangling from a cliff, then about to be carved up by the serial killer or devoured by the dragon – describe her situation using the senses. End the scene there.

The next scene starts where the previous one left off, and shows how your heroine manages to pull herself up the cliff, escape the serial killer, or defeat the dragon. She may achieve this on her own, or with help from a rescuer.

RAISE THE TENSION HIGHER STILL

If your novel uses multiple points of view – that is, one PoV per scene, but not the same for the whole novel – you can raise the tension to almost unbearable levels. Leave the heroine hanging from the cliff and switch to a different PoV, showing what someone else is doing somewhere else, if possible something connected to the cliffhanger situation. This could be a police officer investigating the heroine's abduction, or the distraught husband discovering his wife's disappearance.

Then, in the scene after that, you return to your heroine in peril, and show her rescue.

Not every scene needs a cliffhanger handing, but you can use several in your novel, especially at the end of a chapter.

If you're working on a thriller, your readers will love your cliffhangers.

DRAWBACKS

If you show your PoV in peril at the end of the scene, you need to show how she gets out of it. Show this as live action, not in summary. Readers feel cheated by summaries like "Helga massaged her bruises from yesterday's misadventure. She had been lucky to be rescued by a passing ranger."

Authors of book series sometimes end each book with a cliffhanger, so the reader has to buy the sequel to find out what happens next. This is a dangerous strategy. Some readers, impatient to continue, will buy the next book at once. But other readers will feel frustrated to be left dangling with an unresolved situation. They may hate the author for cheating them and write scathing reviews.

It may be better to end the book with the acute danger over and the book's main conflict resolved, and to keep the reader in suspense with a character hook.

CHAPTER 17: VILLAINS AND MONSTERS

Most novels and short stories have an antagonist (someone who opposes the protagonist), and this person or creature is often dangerous and perhaps evil. This gives you the chance to scare your readers with every encounter.

SLOW INCREASE

The first time your heroine meets the villain, she may not find him very frightening. He may even come across as a kind, pleasant guy, and you may want to fool your reader into believing he can be trusted. Instead of using scare techniques, plant hints in the reader's mind, so subtle that they don't give away the villain's true nature. Euphonics for "foreboding" (see 11 *Euphonics*) can work well.

VOICE

Describe what the villain's voice sounds like. Similes (comparing the voice to another sound) work well, especially if the comparison is something dangerous. Here are examples from my own fiction:

Kirral's voice had the soft scraping tone of a sword grinding against a whetstone.

His voice had the low-humming hiss of a wasp hovering over rotting fruit.

...with the shrill and persistent like a dentist's drill

You can use this technique several times in your novel, as long as you use different descriptions.

SMILE

An evil villain's smile can send chills sliding down the reader's spine. Make the most of it. Don't just write "He smiled." Instead, devote a full sentence to describing this smile:

His eyes lit, and his lips curved in malicious pleasure.

The corners of her mouth turned up.

His smile bared large, glistening teeth.

His upper lip curled with mirth.

Her face slid into an insincere smile.

Use this technique sparingly. The villain's smile has the greatest impact if he smiles only this once. If he smiles all the time, the effect wears off.

HANDS AND CLAWS

Describe the villain's or monster's hands or paws, their colour and texture, the way they move, the shape of the nails or claws.

Are the hands bronzed or pale, wrinkled or smooth? Are the fingers long or pudgy? Are the nails splintered and dirty or perfectly manicured? Are the monster's paws webbed or scaled?

In many people's subconscious, long fingernails create unease, so consider giving your villain longer than average nails. However, male villains with very long nails are a cliché of horror flicks, so don't overdo it.

EYES

Describe the villain's or monster's eyes. A simile works well for conveying the colour, as long as you choose it from your novel's world.

His eyes had the colour of a stagnant pond: dangerous, murky and deep.

...frostbite-coloured eyes

....eyes as grey and cold as street ice

...with a sharp glare from her steel-grey eyes

The pupils in her sapphire eyes narrowed to pinpricks.

...sulphurous yellow with night-dark centres

The topaz eyes did not blink.

....eyes like shiny black beetles

....piercing and deadly like two well-sharpened dirks

NOBILITY

The best villains are not pure evil, but have a genuinely noble side to them. What is your villain's noble feature? Perhaps he does everything in his power to protect children. Maybe he is scrupulously honest and will never speak a lie. Better still, he acts for a cause he believes to be noble, so by his standards, he's doing good deeds.

During the scariest hero/villain confrontation (probably during the novel's climax), show the villain's noble side. This will raise the hero's and the reader's hopes that the villain can be reasoned with (a hope you and the villain will of course dash before long) thus increasing the suspense.

MOVEMENT

Describe the villain's movements. Slow, deliberate movements create the greatest suspense. Be careful not to overuse the words "slowly" and "slow".

SMELLS

What does the villain smell of? Peppermint toothpaste and coal tar soap? Mothballs and old sweat? Bubble gum and lemon shampoo? If the monster is an animal, there may be smells of musk or damp fur, and its breath may smell of rotting meat.

CLICHÉS TO AVOID

Don't give your human villain hot, stinking breath. Every villain who tries to have his way with the heroine in romance novels seems to have halitosis. Let his mouth smell of nicotine or minty mouthwash instead.

Avoid the maniacal evil laughter ("Brua-ha-ha-haw"), a stock ingredient of 20th century pulp fiction. When your villain laughs, it may sound like soft strings tinkling – or he may never laugh at all.

CHAPTER 18: CAPTIVITY

If your protagonist is imprisoned during all or part of a scene, you can make this experience scary.

HOW TO MAKE IT SCARY

If possible, make the room dark. There's no light in the dungeon. If the prison cell has a window, it's high up and narrow, letting in scarce light. The villain has shut off the power supply.

Solitary confinement is scariest. If your heroine is alone in that room, with nobody to talk to, the reader worries for her. She may shout "Is anyone out there? Can you hear me?" and get no reply. Alternatively, she may have a companion in her captivity – until that person gets led away for execution.

Let it be cold. The place is unheated, the protagonist is not wearing many clothes, the air is chilly, the concrete floor is cold, and if a blanket is provided at all it is much too thin.

SENSES

While your protagonist suffers captivity, use the senses a lot.

Hearing (use this sense a lot)
- Rodents' feet
- Shuffling straw
- Fellow captive's sobs and snores
- Agonised screams from another cell

- Clanking door
- Rattling keys
- Screeching lock
- Guard's boots thudding outside
- Seeing (use this sense sparingly)
- Barely visible shapes in the darkness
- Rapidly moving rodents
- Sliver of light from the window
- Crack of light through gap below door

Smelling (very effective, but a little goes a long way)

- Sour stench of urine
- Excrement from previous prisoners
- Old sweat
- Blood
- Rodent excrement
- Rotten straw
- Mould
- Food

Touching (use this sense as much as the scene allows, especially if it's dark)

- The fetters/handcuffs/bonds chafing at the wrists/ankles
- Pain from bruises
- The texture of the wall
- Texture of the door
- Cold hard floor
- Rough blanket
- Cobwebs

- Sodden straw
- Chilly air

<u>Tasting</u> (This may not be relevant)

- The gag in the protagonist's mouth
- The food (may be low standard in a dungeon, but she's probably hungry so it will not taste so bad)

REVULSION

Prisons and dungeons can be disgusting places. You can create a sense of revulsion (see Chapter 1 *Flavours of Fear*) to enhance the reader's fear. This is best achieved by describing smells.

THINKING

While your protagonist is imprisoned, she can't do much beyond explore her surroundings in search of a way out. She will probably think a lot. When sharing her thoughts and feelings, make sure she doesn't wallow in despair. Although she may feel dejected, she keeps searching a way out. Create a tiny hope, let her plan. Later, this plan will fail, but it's important to show some hope in order to create suspense.

CHAPTER 19: CHASES AND ESCAPES

Chases and escapes, experienced from the point of view of the person who flees from the menace, are exciting and create reader sympathy. Here are some techniques to make them frightening.

POINT OF VIEW

If possible, write the scene from the fleeing person's point of view. This means showing only what this person sees, hears and feels. If the POV character runs for her life, she won't pause to watch her pursuer, so don't describe what the pursuer looks like, or how the distance between gradually closes. However, you can describe the sounds the pursuer makes: boots thudding on the asphalt, clanking armour, yells, curses.

PACING

Chases are fast-paced, so use fast-pace writing techniques: short paragraphs, short sentences, short words. But if the chase or escape spreads over more than a few paragraphs, try to vary the pace. This will make it more exciting. When she runs fast, use very short sentences - even sentence fragments - and mostly single-syllabic words. They create a sense of breathlessness and fear. When she's hiding, when she's struggling to climb up a facade inch by inch, when the pursuers have trapped her and when the policeman handcuffs her, use medium-length sentences and words. You can increase the sense of speed by using euphonic effects, especially words containing the letter R.

For more suggestions, see Chapter 10 *Pacing*.

READER SYMPATHY

The reader's sympathy always lies with the fleeing person. You can increase this effect if several people are hounding the refugee. Nothing stirs reader emotion more than a situation of many against one. If possible, build tension by introducing the other pursuers gradually. At first, she runs only from one foe. Just when she thinks she may get away, one of the villain's henchmen comes from another alley. And then a third. In addition, you can give the pursuer advantages over the refugee: physical health, weapons, technology.

If you want to reader to sympathise with the pursuer, show the fugitive using unnecessary violence against an innocent bystander.

DANGER FROM THE SURROUNDINGS

Increase the tension by shifting the action to increasingly dangerous ground. As your heroine flees from the evil villain, she moves towards quicksand, a crumbling bridge, a cliff edge or a ravine. Now she must decide rapidly which poses the greater danger – pursuer or location – and take the risk.

STUMBLING

When a person runs from danger, a cocktail of chemicals gets released in the brain. It includes adrenalin and other substances which dull pain and give stamina but also impair motor skills. Your heroine's movements won't be as coordinated as they usually are, so she may miss her footing, stumble or slip. This is all the more likely because in her hurry, she won't examine the ground where she's treading.

PHYSICAL SYMPTOMS

The running person is probably out of breath, struggling to get enough oxygen. Her chest may feel like it's about to burst. Her heart thuds loudly, not only in her chest but in her head. This thudding continues even when she stops running, and while she's hiding, the heartbeat in her head may be the loudest noise she hears.

EUPHONICS

Certain sounds have certain psychological effects on the reader's mind. While she sees the mob approaching but doesn't yet realise they're after her, or when she senses that something is wrong but does not yet realise the danger she's in, use OW sounds to create foreboding. When she realises they're after her, use TR sounds to convey there's trouble in store. When she runs, use R sounds to convey hurry, perhaps combined with EE for acute fear. Whenever she thinks she may get away, use H. If she is safe, use J and CH for relief and joy, but if they defeat her, use D for a sense of dejection.

PUT UP A FIGHT

When the pursuer catches up with her, she puts up a fight. She does not need to win, but readers will respect her if she manages to inflict some hurt on him before he overpowers her. This is better than if she surrenders meekly, or if she faints and comes to in the dungeon.

CHAPTER 20: VIOLENCE AND GORE

A scene does not need to be violent to be scary. This depends on your personal taste, your genre, and your readers' expectations.

PERSONAL TASTE

Do you enjoy reading gory fiction, with graphic descriptions of violence, with chainsaw massacres and disembowellings? Then write it, and include detailed descriptions of the injuries.

Does the mere mention of violence repulse you? Do you get sick at the sight of blood? When watching a horror movie, do you fast-forward through the gory bits? Then keep descriptions of violence brief and leave out the gruesome detail. Instead, focus on the psychological aspects.

GENRE

Some genres – especially thrillers and full-length horror fiction – practically demand violence, because this is what readers expect, so you need to provide it, although not in every scene.

In a thriller, few scenes contain violence, but the violence is graphic. Descriptions of murder victims are graphic, too, often with details intended to shock.

The horror genre spans a wide range. On one end, psychological horror may show no violence at all, although the threat of it is present; the readers know something terrible is going to happen but they don't witness it on the page. At the other end is slash & gore horror, filled with brutal murders and mutilations, chainsaw massacres and mounds of gore.

In children's fiction and romance, there is little violence and no gore.

READER EXPECTATIONS

Readers expect a certain amount of violence – a lot, a little or none – depending on the genre, on other books by the same author, the book description and the cover picture. If you give them too much for their taste, they'll be grossed out; if you give them too little, they'll be disappointed.

While you can't get it right for everyone, you need to get it right for your average reader. Visualise the typical person buying your book, and consider what other books she has read and who her favourite authors are. Use those as a yardstick for the violence level in your own writing.

In the age of the ebook, readers download sample pages before buying. Try to include in your first pages a hint of the level of violence to come.

The book's blurb (short description on the back cover or the product page) can also give readers a clue. Use phrases such as "extreme horror", "violent" and "not recommended for young readers" to warn potential buyers that this may not be the right book for them.

STRIKING A BALANCE

While violence can create many different kinds of fear, gore creates horror, shock and revulsion.

If you choose to write gory fiction, take care not to create a non-stop gore-fest. Mutilated corpses piling up in scene after scene soon become boring. The impact of gore soon wears off. Also remember that the mental states of horror and shock don't last long; they may give way to indifference. Revulsion is stimulating only if it is brief; continued revulsion puts readers off and sends them in search of something more pleasant.

The trick is to use violence and gore only in some scenes, not all the time. Give the reader the chance to recover between each slaughter, so they're able to experience the horror afresh.

Think of gore as spice: it enhances the flavour of the dish, but is not a dish in itself. Sprinkling black pepper on a dish makes the food more exciting, but you wouldn't enjoy a dish consisting mostly of black pepper and not much else.

USING GORE TO CREATE HORROR

If you want some shock, horror or revulsion but not too much, make the descriptions graphic but keep them short, perhaps just a sentence or two.

To create horror, describe the colours, textures, shapes and movements of the corpses, injuries and horrible things. Describe one or two details rather than the whole thing. Show the white maggots wiggling in the wound, the blood spurting in a wide arc from the shoulder where the limb has been severed, the eyeball hanging by a thread from its socket.

You can increase the horror further by mentioning something innocuous in the same sentence as the gory detail: Blood drips from the ceiling and forms dark patches on the baby blanket. Intestines spill across the lace tablecloth.

A related technique is to use similes, comparing the terrible thing to something innocuous: Blood stains her lace shawl with pink and scarlet like a garden of roses. Guts spill from his abdomen like strings of undigested sausages.

My advice: Make the gore graphic and intense, but use it sparingly and keep it short.

CHAPTER 21: HUMOUR

Humour can work well with horror fiction, creating a contrast that emphasises the horrific, making it even more terrible. At the same time it provides a valve for tension, welcome relief for readers who could otherwise not bear to read on.

When horror mixes with hilarity, the reader guffaws with laughter and at the same time gasps with fear. Aim for macabre or grotesque effects.

Humour is highly personal. What makes one reader convulse in laughter won't even make another's lips twitch. Invite your readers to laugh, but don't expect that all of them will.

Don't force the humour. Adding jokes and slapstick situations to scary scenes works only if you write comedy.

Instead, use a familiar element – something harmless – from earlier in the book; place it into the scary context, perhaps even in a way which makes the situation worse for the hero.

This contrast between the familiar and the gruesome tickles reader's laughter muscles at the same time as it increases their fear.

Example

Let's say Joe, aged 13, has a small dog named Fido. In the book's earlier chapters, he invested great effort into training Fido to kick a ball. We've seen him show Fido how to do it, experimenting with different balls, rewarding him for getting it almost right. But Fido never quite caught on. To Joe's frustration, Fido never kicked hard enough to play football (American: "soccer").

In the scary scene, the Villain is dismembering a body in the garden shed. Hidden in the shed, behind piles of clutter, are Fido and Joe.

Joe's heart thuds in his throat, and his stomach heaves with terror. If the villain spots him, he'll be dead. The reader is in great suspense, wondering if Joe – and Fido – can keep completely still.

At last, the villain has finished his handiwork. He bags up the body parts, wipes the blood from his hands, opens the door and is about to leave.... when Fido spots a ball! This time Fido kicks it the way Joe taught him to, with real strength – straight at the villain's calves.

The reader's reaction is "Oh nooooo!" The reaction mixes laughter with a horrified groan.

CHAPTER 22: BACKLOADING

Here is a nifty technique to give your writing style more impact. It works for all kinds of writing – prose and poetry, fiction and non-fiction, romance and horror – and is perfect for scary scenes.

PUT THE BEST WORD LAST

This means structuring your sentences so the most powerful word comes at the end. The last word touches the reader's psyche more than any other, so make it count.

Short, evocative nouns, adjectives and verbs are best. Here's a list for your inspiration: *death, dead, kill, blood, fear, die, deep, cold, heat, love, dark, boil, pull, grave, grip, grasp, hope, sear, scream, thrill, scar, bone, flesh, skull, fear, wound, pray, pain, soul, child, flee, trap, teeth.*

These words, on the other hand, have no particular effect: *it, then, them, across, through, there, under, of, off, for, that, be, others, him, her.*

Often, restructuring the sentence is all it takes, or perhaps adding, deleting or replacing one word.

Before

She knew she had to kill it.

After

She knew she had to kill.

Before

A corpse lay on the table.

After

On the table lay a corpse.

Before

She had a painful headache.

After

Pain pounded in her skull.

Before

He felt the pain then.

After

Then he felt the pain.

Before

A child was in there.

After

In there was a child.

You don't need to backload every single sentence in your manuscript. Backload the last sentence of some paragraphs, including the last sentence of the scene, because that's where the impact is greatest.

EXAMPLES FROM BOOKS

Many bestselling authors use this technique, either consciously or by instinct. Here are some random sentences (all at the end of paragraphs) from books by famous authors:

- Thomas Harris: *Red Dragon*

  Far out by the tidal flats, bait fish leaped for their lives.

- Tania Carver, *The Creeper*

  They looked like two open, ragged wounds.

- Lisa Gardner: *The Killing Hour*

  But she and Mandy had come to understand early on that he mostly belonged to the dead.

- Angela Carter: *The Lady of the House of Love*

  Sometimes the countess will wake it for a brief cadenza by strumming the bars of its cage; she likes to hear it announce how it cannot escape.

- Tanith Lee: *When The Clock Strikes*

  Like the prophecy of the clock, it was a subject for the dark.

- Tanith Lee, *Pied Piper*

  Even though he was a god, a god of love.

BACKLOADING SCENES

As well as putting a powerful word at the end of a sentence, you can put a powerful sentence at the end of your scene. This really stirs the reader's emotions.

Similarly, you can backload the end of your short story or novel with a powerful sentence. Short sentences with evocative words work best for this.

CHAPTER 23: THE STORY'S FIRST AND FINAL SCENES

Are you creating a scary scene for the beginning or the ending of your work? Here are some tips you may want to consider.

START WITH SUSPENSE, NOT TERROR

Inexperienced horror writers often open their story with a situation of extreme terror, hoping to shock the readers. This does not work.

Readers don't feel extreme emotions (terror, horror, panic, shock) until they have become involved in the story and care for the character. Therefore, those gruesome openings have no effect.

Extreme openings have another drawback: it's almost impossible to build up from there. If the monster guts a dozen women and eats their babies in the first paragraph, everything that comes after will fall flat.

Instead, I recommend starting your story with the subtler forms of fear.

Suspense is best. The more suspense you can create on the first page, the better. This applies to all genres, and to novels as well as to short stories.

If you're writing a thriller, a horror novel or an urban fantasy, you can supplement the suspense with apprehension, anxiety, foreboding and unease. See Chapter 1 *Flavours of Fear.*

AVOID CLICHED BEGINNINGS

Some horror openings have been used so many times, they make readers yawn. Agents and editors receive so many manuscripts with these openings in the slush pile – often several every day – that this leads to automatic rejections.

Horror openings over-used by beginner writers

1. The author sits at the computer, writing a story, and suddenly the invented monsters become real and threaten the writer.

2. The painter stands at the easel, painting a picture, and suddenly the painted monsters become real and threaten the artist.

ENDINGS – FEAR OR NOT?

Do you want to conclude your work with a scene which really scares your readers? This may be a good strategy – or not. It depends on the genre, and above all, on the length of the work.

With a short story, scary endings are good. If you can leave your readers frightened after they've finished reading, you have achieved something great. You can load the final paragraphs with any flavour of fear including horror, terror, unease, foreboding or shock. If your reader is frightened to turn off the light, then you have achieved your end goal. You can even kill your main character in the last paragraph.

But with a novel, the situation is different. The reader has spent a lot of time identifying with the main character; she wants that person to be safe. If you kill the heroine at the end, the reader may not forgive you. Having invested intense feelings in the novel – including intense fears – the reader expects an emotional pay-off. She wants the feeling of satisfaction and relief, and you had better deliver those if you want her to buy your next book. With thrillers and horror novels, it's okay to leave the reader with residues of fear, perhaps a sense of unease, or suspense about what will happen in the sequel. In other genres, especially romance, the final scene should not create any fear at all.

POSSIBLE ENDINGS FOR HORROR FICTION

1. The hero defeats the monster. This works well for novels. It is satisfying and gives the reader the relief she craves.

2. The hero defeats the monster, but wonders if the price was too high. This works for many novels (except romance), novellas and long stories.

3. The monster defeats the hero. This ending is recommended only for the horror genre and only for short stories.

4. The hero defeats the monster, but it was only a minor monster. The real monster is just stirring. This can be effective in short stories and in some novels, especially in the horror genre. It opens the door to a possible sequel.

5. The hero defeats the monster – and realising that in doing so, he has unleashed greater evil. This is good for short stories, and can also be effective in horror and fantasy novels.

6. The hero defeats the monster – but regrets it. This can have powerful impact in short stories, and can also work in some novels, especially fantasy.

TWIST ENDINGS

Stories ending with a twist in the tail are perfect for horror. However, almost everything has been done before, and it's almost impossible to invent a new twist. So when you use a twist ending, don't rely on the surprise, and make sure you're giving your reader something meaningful beyond the twist.

AVOID ANTICLIMACTIC ENDINGS

Keeping the tension high is one of the main challenges of the horror genre. Once the reader has seen the monster face-to-face, or once a terrible situation has scared her out of her serenity, anything else is a let-down. This is especially tricky with endings, because you need to end the story on a strong note.

With a thriller, you can achieve this by moving the scary climax close to the end, so the reader gets the earned relief while the heart still races from the frightening experience. If you write romance, this is no problem at all; work on the reader's other emotions to create a satisfying, intense ending.

But with horror, creating a satisfying ending is difficult. Whatever you choose for your ending, avoid the total anticlimax. If readers find out at the end that there was no real reason for fear, they may throw the book against the wall in disgust, and not read anything by this author again.

Anticlimactic endings to avoid

1. The monster isn't a monster but a harmless pet/friendly alien.

2. The villain isn't evil but is actually the hero's anonymous supporter/the long-lost loving mother/Jesus Christ.

3. The experience was only a dream/only a simulation/only a computer game.

CHAPTER 24: BLACK MOMENT AND CLIMAX SCENES

When plotting your novel, you probably created – consciously or instinctively – a "black moment" scene and a "climax" scene.

THE BLACK MOMENT

About two-thirds into the book, all seems lost. The hero is under pressure and close to giving up. Internal and external conflicts have increased to the degree that your hero can't bear it any more. His girlfriend has broken up with him, his allies have deserted the cause, he has been fired from his job and evicted from his home, the villain's henchmen are closing in, and his big secret has been exposed in the press. Under pressure, he is close to giving up. To make matters worse, his girl has been abducted and will die unless the hero surrenders the proof of the villain's machinations... and he can neither rescue her nor deliver the documents because he's locked up in a prison cell.

The hero feels rage, despair and a whole cocktail of other emotions. Consider adding fear: he fears for himself as well as for the safety of his abducted girlfriend, for the city the villain is about to bomb to dust, or for the survival of the human race.

Turn the suspense volume up as high as you can. Dread, revulsion, horror or panic can also work well.

Try to use a "ticking clock" in this scene, especially if you're writing a thriller. See Chapter 8 *Keep the Clock Ticking*.

If you can, isolate the hero from his remaining supporters and put him in a situation where he cannot call for help. See Chapter 6 *Total Isolation*.

Other good techniques for the black moment are in Chapters 4 *Dark and Dangerous*, 9 *Feel the Fear* and 18 *Captivity*.

THE CLIMAX

After the black moment, the hero rallies all his strength and inner resources; he uses his skills, overcomes his deepest fears, and faces the final challenge.

This climax comes near the end of the book: sometimes immediately after the black moment, sometimes a little later. It is the most exciting and scariest scene in the novel.

This is when the final big confrontation between the protagonist (hero/heroine) and the antagonist (villain/monster) takes place. Often, it involves a fight.

Draw out this confrontation, spreading it over one or several scenes. Sometimes it looks like the hero wins, sometimes the villain. Keep the outcome in doubt until the end, so the reader is in suspense throughout. Remind the reader what the hero is fighting for.

Build up to it with suspense, apprehension and anxiety. Then, use an intense kind of fear: terror is an excellent choice if your plot permits.

Strain the reader's nerves to the highest possible extent. Don't hold back!

If your novel contains gory sections, then this scene is the goriest.

Pick a dangerous place for this scene: a sinking ship, a burning building, the edge of a cliff, a dam about to burst. See Chapter 14 *Choosing the Location*.

In romance the climax is about the couple's relationship, and the external danger is secondary. Use the scary situation to apply additional pressure on the couple and to add an extra level of excitement.

Does your hero have an overwhelming fear, perhaps a phobia? In previous scenes, he avoided doing the scary thing. In the climax, however, it's the only way to win; he rallies his strength and faces his fear.

CHAPTER 25: GENRES

Different genres require different treatment of scary scenes. Here are some suggestions.

ROMANCE

Readers buy romance novels because of the love story. They want to be thrilled by the romantic conflicts and erotic tension, not by horror, terror and panic. Scary scenes can enrich a romance novel, but be careful not to overdo it! Use the fearful situations to support, not to compete with, the romance plot. Perhaps the couple had a falling out and she stormed off in anger; now she must face the dangerous situation alone, realising how much better it would be if he were around. Maybe hero and heroine are opponents, fighting for conflicting causes, until a great evil threatens to destroy them and those they love... forcing them to become allies making them realise they can count on each other.

Did you know that in a situation of danger, men are more likely to fall in love with the woman nearest to them than at any other time? If the two have known each other all their lives, and he views her as a good mate and nothing else, then his feelings may change when they are huddled together in the cave while the monster prowls outside.

Focus on the subtle forms of fear, especially suspense and anxiety. Foreboding works well in paranormal romance. Use the intense flavours of fear only if they are appropriate for your sub-genre. Terror, horror or panic can work in action romance and paranormal romance, but are out of place in light regency romance.

The most useful reader-scaring techniques for romance novels are in Chapters 3 *What Lurks Behind That Door,* 4 *Dark and Dangerous,* 7 *Strip to Tease,* 9 *Feel the Fear* and 15 *Using the Senses.*

HUMOUR

When you add scary situations and creepy atmosphere to a funny story, you get black humour. In scary scenes, contrast what the reader expects with what she doesn't expect or the familiar with the unfamiliar. For instance, if a character has done something several times, and he does it again in a situation of danger (perhaps unleashing disaster) this can be hilarious and scary.

Techniques working particularly well in horrible humour or in humorous horror fiction are in Chapters 3 *What Lurks Behind That Door,* 4 *Dark and Dangerous,* 7 *Strip to Tease* and 11 *Euphonics.*

FANTASY

In this genre you can use both the subtle and the intense flavours of fear several times. It may be best to use each of them only once in the book, however – except for suspense and excitement. Use these a lot!

Foreboding and horror are great for epic fantasy, or dread shock and terror for urban fantasy. You can also use revulsion, but sparingly.

Chapters 17 *Villains And Monsters* and 18 *Captivity* may also be useful.

EROTICA

Readers of this genre want to be cosseted and caressed, not grossed out or scared. There may be no really scary scenes. Use mostly suspense, apprehension and excitement and avoid the intense forms of fear altogether.

Erotica involving bondage, dominance, sado-masochism, spanking and playful punishment are different: the fear increases the thrill. It's probably best to stay clear of terror and panic, however, because those would spoil the reader's fun. Instead turn the volume for suspense and apprehension on high.

Useful techniques are in Chapters 4 *Dark and Dangerous,* 7 *Strip To Tease,* 9 *Feel the Fear* and 15 *Using the Senses.*

SCIENCE FICTION

You can use whatever flavour of fear suits your plot best. Suspense, excitement, apprehension, unease and horror work especially well.

HORROR

Readers who buy horror books want to be scared, so give them that thrill. To avoid boring your readers, use all the flavours of fear at different times and vary the intensity.

You may want to use every reader-scaring technique covered in this book. Although you should keep your reader in an almost constant state of fear, a continued stream of equally-horrific frights becomes boring. To keep the tension high, pay attention to Chapter 12 *Peaks and Troughs.*

THRILLER

Give your reader the thrill she craves in a mix of subtle and intense flavours. All forms of fear can work well in thrillers. Dread and terror are best.

The most effective techniques to use are in Chapters 3 *What Lurks Behind That Door,* 4 *Dark and Dangerous,* 6 *Total Isolation,* 8 *Keep the Clock Ticking,* 10 *Pacing,* and 17 *Villains and Monsters.*

COSY MYSTERY

Unlike the thriller readers, the buyer of cosy mysteries does not want to be scared. A slight acceleration of the pulse and a tingling spine are enough for her. Take care not to take her beyond her boundaries or gross her out.

You can use all the subtle forms of fear – suspense, apprehension, foreboding, excitement, unease – but stay clear of the intense ones... although a moment of panic is acceptable.

Great techniques to use are in Chapters 3 *What Lurks Behind That Door* and 8 *Keep the Clock Ticking.*

HISTORICAL

For this genre, you can use any flavour of fear that suits the plot. Apprehension, horror and revulsion work particularly well.

You may also find Chapters 17 *Villains And Monsters* and 18 *Captivity* useful.

LITERARY

Although this genre seldom offers scary scenes, you can add a sprinkling of fear as spice. Apprehension, foreboding and horror can be effective.

YOUNG ADULT

Teenagers love the thrill of a good scare, so go ahead and frighten them. Mix subtle and intense flavours to suit the plot. It may be best to avoid excessive graphic violence, however.

CHILDREN'S FICTION

Young readers love excitement and enjoy a good fictional fight. However, they are not able to appreciate the subtle flavours of fear which require a frame of reference (such as foreboding). On the other hand, children understand suspense - so give them a lot of it.

Among the intense kinds of fear, horror works best. Calibrate the level of horror for your target age group to make sure they can cope. You want the kids to squeal with delighted fear for a moment, not to stay traumatised for a year.

The techniques outlined in Chapter 3 *What Lurks Behind That Door* and 6 *Total Isolation* are perfect for children's fiction.

CHAPTER 26: THE WIMP EFFECT

Now you've made your scene scary, there's the danger that your protagonist comes across as a wimpy wuss.

Readers don't like wusses.

Heroes may be frightened, but they may not be wusses. Often, the difference lies not in the hero's actions, but in the words you've used.

You may have created a spunky, heroic, brave heroine, but the reader still perceives her as a wimpy wuss, because you've unwittingly used certain phrases which signal "wimp" to the reader's subconscious. I call this the Wimp Effect.

It's best to avoid those words, or at least, to use them sparingly.

THE WIMP TEST

If you like, apply the following test to your scary scene, and see how your heroine or hero performs. Every time your protagonist does one of the following things, she or he gets one Wimp Point.

- Sighing, exhaling, breath taking. Each time the protagonist heaves a sigh, sighs deeply, takes a deep breath, inhales, exhales slowly etc, that's one Wimp Point.

- Shrugging. Shrugs may be intended to convey arrogance or indifference, but they also signal weakness. One Wimp Point for each shrug.

- Hesitation. Each time the protagonist hesitates, however good the reason, that's a Wimp Point.

- Visceral responses to minor triggers. Visceral responses to real danger are great! But if the protagonist shudders, trembles, jerks and gasps at something harmless like the sound of a banging door, this gets a Wimp Point.

- Indulging in negative-passive emotions. It's okay to feel sadness, grief, loss, worry, anxiety, helplessness. However, these should be dealt with quickly. The protagonist should experience them but not dwell on them. Each time such an emotion is described for more than one sentence, it gets a Wimp Point.

- Tears. Each time the protagonist weeps, spills tears, wipes a tear from his eyes, gets moist eyes, or has a tear sliding down her cheek, earns one Wimp Point.

- Thinking. Thoughts should be very, very short, or implied in the action. Whenever the protagonist thinks for more than one sentence, that's a Wimp Point. If he thinks aloud, or holds conversations with himself, the Wimp Points double.

- Nervous habits. Each time the protagonist bites or chews lips, cheeks or nails, clenches fists or teeth, freezes, gulps, swallows, clears a throat, drops a jaw or stares in disbelief, that's one Wimp Point.

- Tries and attempts. Each time your protagonist tries (or "attempts" or "endeavours") something, that's one Wimp Point. When he tries something in connection with an emotional response (*He tried not to shudder. She tried to suppress a groan. He couldn't stop himself trembling*), the points double.

- Feeling. Every time the word "feel" is used. (*He felt xxx. Feeling yyy, she did zzz*)

- Finding themselves. Every time the protagonist finds himself in a place or situation (He found himself in a dark alleyway), or finds himself doing something instead of doing it (*He found himself shaking all over. She found herself staring at a house)*, this earns one Wimp Point.

- Involuntary actions. Each time she does something "involuntarily", "unconsciously", "instinctively", "without meaning to" or "against her will", it gets one Wimp Point.

- Each time the protagonist's body parts (instead of the protagonist) do something *(His legs stepped forward. His hands took the weapon. Her eyes watched the rat.)* gets one Wimp Point.

How many Wimp Points has the protagonist earned? Aim for no more than three in your scariest scene, and no more than ten or fifteen in the whole book, although it depends on the genre. Romance can be allowed a little more; thrillers fewer. Females are allowed a few more points than males, but not many more.

Some writers accumulate a dozen Wimp Points in a single paragraph, and are surprised when readers don't think their heroine is spunky.

Here are examples of how a section with many Wimp Points might read.

Wimp Example 1

Henry Hero stared in disbelief at the dark river, and couldn't help himself swallowing. He found himself shaking involuntarily. Part of him whispered, No man has ever crossed this sea alive. Go home while you can. *Another part of him yelled,* Just do it. Be the First. *He chewed his lower lip, hesitating. A cloud crossed the sky, making him shudder. Then he took a deep breath to steady himself, and exhaled with a sigh.* I have to do it, *he told himself.* The Delectable Damsel needs me. *His feet stepped towards the shore.*

Wimp Example 2

Captain Hero stared at the starship's monitor, disbelieving, and swallowed. That's the end, *part of him said.* There's nothing you can do. *Another part of him said,* Don't just stand there. Do something. *The first part of him replied,* It's hopeless. In thirty seconds, this ship is going to blow up in a ball of fire. *The second part continued,* But how you use those thirty seconds matters. *He found himself trembling against his will. He chewed his lower lip and heaved a sigh, wondering how he should spend the final moments of his life.*

Without meaning to, he found himself looking at a pretty crying yeoman. His legs walked towards her. He hesitated for a second, then he took a deep breath. *His arms stretched to pull her close, and he found himself hugging her.*

Part of him said, It's against the rules to make love to a member of his crew, *but another part of him said,* It doesn't matter any more. *He couldn't stop himself sighing deeply. Duty comes first, he told himself. He took a deep breath to steady himself. Then he swallowed, and returned to the console.*

SOME WIMP POINTS ARE OKAY

Each of the "Wimp Effects" is fine on its own, if it happens just once. A single sigh, a single swallow, a one-off burst into tears are fine.

It's when the Wimp Points accumulate that they become problematic, and they accumulate quickly. Novice writers often have twenty or more Wimp Points in the first chapter, because their characters "shrug" and "sigh" constantly. This establishes their protagonists as wusses before the scary action begins.

The hero Odysseus weeps several times in Homer's epic *The Odyssey.* Does this make him a wimp? Definitely not. The weeping shows him as a sensitive human, and it works because he doesn't do anything else to earn Wimp Points. He doesn't sigh, shrug, inhale, exhale, bite his lips and clear his throat. If he did all those things on top of the weeping, he would come across as a wuss, no matter how many cyclops and monsters he defeated.

It also depends on the character. A timid character is allowed the occasional Wimp Point, but not many.

Examples:
- Spunky person: *She halted.* (0 Wimp Points)
- Timid person: *She hesitated.* (1 Wimp Point)
- Wimpy wuss: *She hesitated, chewing her lips, and heaved a deep sigh.* (3 Wimp Points)
- Spunky person: *She braced herself.* (0 Wimp Points)

- Timid person: *She swallowed and braced herself.* (1 Wimp Point)
- Wimpy wuss: *She swallowed. Then she took a deep breath, exhaled slowly, and braced herself.* (4 Wimp Points)

HOW TO AVOID THE WIMP EFFECT

Wherever possible, cut down on Wimp Points. Delete sighs, shrugs, inhales, exhales, lip biting, cheek chewing, swallowing etc.

Don't let your protagonists do a lot of thinking, and never let two parts of their psyche engage in a conversation.

If the plot demands that the protagonist hesitates, express it with different words *(He halted. He paused. He waited)*

If the protagonist tries to do something, express it without the words "try", "attempt", "endeavour". Instead of *He tried to pull it out* write *He pulled at it with all his strength.*

Describe negative-passive emotions intensely but briefly.

STORY EXAMPLES

Here are three of my short stories, all mild (not gory) horror. See if you can recognise which techniques I have employed, and consider whether you would have used different techniques, or the same techniques but in a different way.

DRUID STONES *by Rayne Hall*

Barbed wire laced the top of the narrow gate, and the jagged end of a broken signpost stuck out of the gorse hedge. The owner of the land, it seemed, disliked people using the ancient Right of Way.

But whatever the farmer's quarrels with occasional tourists, modern-day druids or scholars of ancient history, it did not concern Kathy. She had come a long way to Cornwall on her first holiday since the divorce to explore the stone circles, and would not let a stretch of barbed wire stop her.

Unhooking the stiff latch, she allowed the gate to screech open. She squeezed through the gap, dodging thorny brambles and spider webs. She hated spiders, and no doubt many of them lurked in the dank growth. Hedges towered on either side of the overgrown trail, their branches heavy with water from the earlier rain.

On reaching the stile, she found it also seamed with barbed wire. There was no signpost, not even a broken one. The landowners seemed determine to block a public Right of Way. They might have trouble with vandals, litterers and crop-tramplers, but Kathy was none of these. She never interfered, never meddled, never left more than footprints. She had the right to see the remotest of the ancient monuments, the Dredhek Druid Stones.

Her jeans snagged as she climbed across the barbed stile. At fifty-five, she wasn't as agile as she'd been last time she'd visited stone circles. How long ago had that been? Almost forty years. She'd been on a youth holiday in Cornwall, dating a blond afro-haired boy from the campsite. Not that they'd seen many monuments. They'd been too absorbed necking under the hedgerows.

Whereas these days, Kathy would not miss the chance to experience the ancient magic. The earth energy surrounding Men-at-Tol and at the Merry Maidens had sent her dancing in honour of the elements. What would the Dredhek Druid Stones do to her?

On the other side of the stile, she found nothing but neck-high brambles, nettles, scratchy thistles. No path was in sight. The other stone circles had been easier to get to, even in the rain.

Should she retrace her steps? Perhaps she had taken a wrong turn somewhere, missing a stile or mistaking a plain gate for a kissing gate. The drizzle started again, and the printer's ink on the cheaply produced guidebook ran. Somewhere far away, a dog howled.

Step by step, she trudged across ploughed fields, treading down the thicket of bracken and thorny brambles. Soon, her trouser legs were soaked up to the knees and clods of clay soil clung to her trainers. When she sampled the first blackberries of the season, they tasted acid and gritty, with more pips than sour flesh. It couldn't be much further now, could it?

Suddenly the thicket cleared, as if by sorcery. Below her, twelve stones of grey granite stood chest-high, sticking from the sodden ground like teeth from scurvy gums. What a view! Excited, Kathy quickened her steps, impatient to touch the stones, all twelve of them.

As soon as she placed her hand on the rough surface of the nearest boulder, the ancient energy rose and tingled in her palm. The thirteenth stone, the one in the centre, beckoned strongest. Twice the height of the others, it stood tilted at a phallic angle. Its broad, flat back invited her to lean against it.

Below the overhang of the tilted stone, a posy of wildflowers wilted: yarrow, dandelion and gorse. How touching: someone still worshipped at this ancient site, where people had prayed for thousands of years.

She picked up the blooms. Beneath them lay the charred remains of a frog, its hind legs grotesquely sprawled.

She swallowed the welling sickness. So what if a group of neo-pagans or whatever they were wished to make a burnt offering? Thousands of animals got slaughtered everyday for food, and thousands of frogs got run over on the roads. They'd probably not burnt it alive anyway. Didn't Druids have the custom of triple deaths? They'd probably strangled it first and drained its blood before putting it on the fire. She had no business judging their customs.

As she replaced the flowers to hide the corpse, she recalled a glimpse of a druid ritual during that Cornish holiday decades ago. The memory descended like a damp cloud.

Roaming the fields in search of a private spot, she and Jerry had stumbled across a group of cloaked, hooded figures with sickles and staffs.

The druids, though polite, had made it clear they did not like outsiders watching their ritual. Kathy wanted to leave immediately, but Jerry walked right into the gathering to a pale, red-cloaked woman.

With his bell-bottom trousers and purple striped shirt, Jerry looked pathetic among the robed druids. "Are you all right, lady?" he asked. "Do you need help?"

"Ngnggggg." The woman swayed, staggered, and raised her arms. "Ongengeeee."

"The lady is our queen." The tallest of the druids pointed at her crown of wildflowers and ivy. "She's had a little too much fly agaric, but we're looking after her."

"Engeeeengeeee." The woman's diluted pupils confirmed that she was drugged.

Kathy pulled Jerry's sleeve. "Let's go. This is a private celebration, and they can do what they like. Freedom of religion and all that."

"That's right. Freedom of religion." The tall druid smiled benevolently and drew a sign in the air, not unlike the Christian blessing of the cross.

Still Jerry didn't budge. "She looks sick. She needs help."

"For God's sake, Jerry!" Kathy dragged him away. "This isn't your business. You're embarrassing me."

On their way back to the camp, they argued. Jerry kept worrying about the drugged woman, and Kathy kept telling him the druids knew what they were doing and he had no right to meddle. At last, he fell silent. But there had been no more kissing that night, and after that, their romance had fizzled out.

The memory of that long-ago quarrel, combined with the charred frog, spoilt the magical mood. Dusk was falling anyway: time to leave. A well-trodden path led westward across a ploughed field, probably to a remote country road. Perhaps that was the way she should have come, instead of scrambling across barbed wire fences.

A distant sound alerted her, a chanting like the hum of a coming swarm of bees mingled with the low beat of drums. Six figures approached with large strides, each carrying a staff, their white hooded robes flowing. Bronze sickles gleamed at their waists.

Unwilling to get caught up in another druid ritual, Kathy ducked between a hawthorn hedge and a pile of firewood part-covered with a green tarpaulin, to let them pass. Her trousers grew sodden and her legs cold. All around her thick, sticky spider threads hung with raindrops like glass-bead necklaces.

But the procession halted before the stone circle. They rammed torches into the ground. Soon, the flames hissed in the damp air.

If she crawled out of the undergrowth now, it would look as if she had been spying on their ritual. To avoid the embarrassment, she would have to stay hidden until they were done.

A tall man with a circlet on his head chuckled. "I wonder what the Red Goddess will send us as an offering this year."

"Something small, I hope," a woman piped up. "A mouse or a rabbit. The sheep last year took ages to bleed out, and then it wouldn't burn."

"This time, I've brought enough wood for a big animal." The man pointed to the tarpaulin-covered pile.

He intoned an invocation of the Red Goddess, his voice deep and resonant like that of the solo baritone in Kathy's church choir.

Damp chills crawled up Kathy's calves and her thighs cramped. Rain trickled from a hawthorn bough into her collar and slid down her spine, but she held still. The ritual could not take much longer.

Now the druids strode in a clockwise circle, stepping across the part-exposed stones. Splashes of mud soiled their pristine white robes.

"Summer's gifts, summer's sacrifice...." Their chant, low and musical, had a hypnotic quality.

The inside of Kathy's wrist tickled. A fat spider with striped legs was crawling into her sleeve. She squealed.

At once, a druid strode to her hedge and pointed his staff at her like a spear. His young pimply face shaped into a grin. "See what I've found hiding in the haws."

Kathy's heart hammered in her chest. "I'm sorry, I...I didn't mean to... I don't want to disturb you or to interfere or anything..."

He pulled her up by the wrist and hauled her into the circle.

"Now, now," the druid with the circlet chided. "Let's treat our guest with courtesy." To Kathy, he said, "If you wish to be part of our ritual, you're welcome."

"But-" One of the females frowned up at him.

He silenced her with an impatient flick of his sickle. "I'm in charge here." His voice had a sharp edge. "It is through me the ancient blood flows, through me the gods speak. Never forget that."

"It's all right," Kathy said hastily. "I really don't want to bother you. I ought to go, anyway."

"You're welcome to stay," the chief druid said. "Very welcome indeed. We celebrate Lughnasad, the ancient festival of the first harvest. Have some wine."

He offered her an earthenware cup.

"If you're sure you don't mind me watching your celebration." She took the clay beaker from his manicured fingers and sipped. It tasted odd. Probably a home-brewed herbal concoction.

"Drink all of it," he instructed in the tone of a dentist telling a patient to rinse her mouth.

The brew was potent, almost instantly stirring a dizzy spin in her head. Gratefully, she accepted a chunk of bread, broken from a plaited loaf, still fragrant from baking.

The druid pointed the staff at her. "Denims are not appropriate for a high festival."

"Sorry. I didn't expect to attend a druid celebration. I'd better go. I don't want to ruin your festival with the wrong clothes."

"Stay. We'll loan you a robe."

With a flick of his arm, he commanded the older woman druid, who brought a bulky velvet garment the colour of blood, with a hole in the head and holes for the arms.

"Thanks, but I'd rather not." Kathy struggled against the growing unease. "You've been very kind, I don't belong here."

All six drew close around her, chanting in low murmurs. Kathy struggled in vain as he pinned her arm to her back while another forced the red robe over her head.

The chief druid ripped the tarpaulin off the pyre and poured the contents of a canister. Petrol stink spread. Then a match scraped. Flames shot up, cackled and hissed.

"Lughnasad is the time of the year when tradition demands a sacrifice to the Red Goddess, to ensure a fertile harvest for the annual cycle. Terrible things happen when people don't obey." The chief druid strode up to Kathy and bent to peer into her face. She could smell the mint on his breath. He pressed a wreath of ivy on her scalp. "You're very welcome to join our ritual."

Kathy fought to break free.

A needle-sharp pain stabbed into her cheek, and again.

The younger female druid clutched the big pendant on her chest. "My former grove only ever used flowers and fruit. A rabbit, I can understand. Even a sheep. But -"

"This is my grove." The chief druid tapped his staff on the rock beneath his feet. "I make the decisions. This is how our grove has sacrificed for millennia; this is how we shall continue."

The young druid with gangly limbs fidgeted with his hood. "Won't she be missed? There'll be people looking for her."

The chief held up his arms. "The gods speak through me. This creature is alone here. She is alone in life. She is the offering the gods desire. Do you dare disobey the gods?"

Kathy's mouth was swelling with numbness, like at the dentists. Dizziness clouded her mind, and her willpower seeped away. Her body sagged against the leaning centre stone. The rock's ancient chill seeped into her bones.

The chief took the sickle and caressed its blade. It gleamed in the torchlight. "You won't feel much pain when I cut your wrists," he assured her, using the same tone as a dentist telling a patient it would hurt just a little. "You'll be pleasantly tired and whoozy. We'll drain your blood, and strangle you, and then before you expire, we'll put you on the pyre for burning. Have some more wine and poppy juice."

"Hey, those kids are watching!" The pimply druid pointed his staff at a clump of gorse.

Kathy twisted in her captor's tight grip to see a pair of curly-haired teenagers in flaring jeans. Rescue had arrived.

"Help me," she tried to call, but the sounds squeezing from her swollen mouth came out as "Ngnggg. Ongengeee."

The chief druid's hands clasped her arms like iron grips. "The lady is our queen. She's had a little too much fly agaric, but we're looking after her."

"Engeeeengeeee," Kathy pleaded desperately, imploring them with her eyes.

But the girl was pulling the boy away. "Let's go. This is a private celebration, and they can do what they like." She sounded embarrassed. "Freedom of religion and all that."

"That's right. Freedom of religion," the chief druid said. She felt his breath on her neck and smelled his minty toothpaste again.

The boy, bless him, seemed to sense that something was wrong. "She looks sick. She needs help."

"For God's sake, Jerry!" Even as Kathy implored them with her eyes, the girl was leaving, pulling the boy after her. "This isn't your business. You're embarrassing me."

In numbed disbelief, Kathy watched them walk away. The curly-haired boy once glanced back over his shoulder, then they were gone.

THROUGH THE TUNNEL *by Rayne Hall*

"Is this your idea of a date?" I asked. "Driving from one motorbike shop to another?"

"The next one's only ten miles away." Tony slammed into a lower gear and forced the car up the steep road. "You said you liked motorbikes."

All right, I'd said that. I fancied Tony like crazy and would have claimed to like yellow toads if that got me his attention. And when he suggested driving around the country stopping in a few places, I'd jumped at the chance to spend a day with him. But then I always rush into things which seem a good idea at the time.

"You didn't say we'd be looking at motorbikes all the time," I grumbled.

"Well, what did you expect?" he snapped.

What did a city girl expect from a day out in the country? Picnic in a flowery meadow, surrounded by frolicking lambs. Holding hands by a bubbling brook while the birds twittered in the branches above and the high firs of the forest rustled in the distance. Not looking at one motorbike shop after another. Heavens, I had no idea the countryside was littered with them!

Tony admired the Suzuki's sleek body, the Yamaha's spirit, the Harley's class. He barely noticed my very sleek miniskirt and stylish black heels, not even my shapely legs, however decoratively I displayed them,

"I won't go to another motorbike shop," I declared. "Take me home now."

He turned the windscreen wipers on against the new drizzle. "Ok, ok. I'll take you home, sure. As soon as we've seen the Harley Davidson shop."

I had enough. "Let me out at the nearest railway station!"

To my frustration, he did just that. He even leant across me to open the door.

I got out, waited for an expression of regret, and when none came, I yelled "I don't want to hear from you, ever!" and slammed the car door shut.

The motor whined in accelerating anger.

I should have thought about my dramatic exit before I let him disappear. In particular, I should have ascertained where I was. All I knew was that I was surrounded by lots of countryside, far from civilisation as I knew it.

I braced myself against the wind, clutched my little handbag, and strode to the train stop as fast as my high heels would allow. Of course it started to rain in earnest. It always did when I neglected to check the weather forecast.

'Espley' the station sign said, except there was no station, only a platform next to a single track. A solitary, graffiti-smeared plastic box offered little shelter from the wet gusts. It didn't even have seats, only a ticket machine which said 'Out of Order.' The timetable on the shelter wall was covered with yellowed plastic. I deciphered the tiny printed figures. A train would leave Espley at 17.04, any minute now, which, considering my impulsive decision and the weather, was fortunate.

The wind whipped my long hair into my face, raindrops dripped from my nose, and my legs chilled like they'd been placed in a wine cooler.

I glanced along the silvery track, which disappeared into dark forest one way, and into an even darker tunnel the other. I willed the train to come quickly, but it didn't.

A man, young, tall and very wet, came running down the slope on the other side of the track. "Has the train come yet?" he shouted.

Clad in jeans and trainers and carrying a backpack, he jogged across the line.

"The train?" he repeated, panting.

"You're in luck. It should come any minute now. In fact, it should already have been here. 17.04 the timetable says, I think. Wait, I'll look again." I let my finger run along the tiny printed lines. "Yes, 17.04 B. B means –"

My heart sank into my stomach. B meant 'Weekdays only'. Today was Saturday.

"There's no train. None at all today," I croaked. My brain, as always, immediately conjured up a solution. "Let's get a taxi and share it. Do you know a good taxi company around here?"

I opened my purse, fingered the banknotes. Heaven be thanked, I had had the foresight to take money with me. That would have been just like me, leaving the house without cash. I felt generous. "I'll pay for the taxi to the nearest town where a train stops. But I don't have any coins for the phone call, do you?"

The man shook his head. "If you mean to phone from that phone box by the road – that was vandalised a year ago and has never been fixed. I tried earlier."

"Oh, rats." I stalked down to the road to check. All that remained of the phone box was an empty shell. "Rats."

My brain was already presenting a new solution. "We'll hitch a lift."

Of course I knew hitchhiking was dangerous, and that with my high heels, black mini-skirt, lacquered handbag and damp-clinging top, I looked like an invitation to the kind of motorist my mother had warned me about. But in the company of a man I should be safe. "Oh, by the way, I'm Allie. And you?"

"Steve. I wouldn't count on any car coming at all. There's no traffic here on weekends."

"There has to be," I insisted. "Even if there's not much traffic, the'll be cars."

After ten minutes in the whipping wind, with icy rain slashing into my face, my clothes were soaked through, and I had enough. But I waited a full half hour without a vehicle in sight before I admitted defeat.

"We'll have to walk," I declared. "How far is it to the nearest village?"

"There isn't one. Well, a hamlet that way – a mile as the crow flies, or along the railway line through the tunnel. But the road takes ten, eleven miles, because it detours and curves up the mountain."

I'd only ever walked a mile or two, and that with great reluctance. Ten miles on a rising road sounded unmanageable, even if I had practical shoes and dry clothes.

Drizzle slickened the asphalt. The forested slopes greyed behind a wet veil, and bank of heavy cloud stretched across the sky. Still no car came. Not even a motorbike.

"There's a path where I came from." Steve jerked his chin up the mountain. "It goes straight to a viewing platform, where there's a kiosk and toilets in summer. But that's all closed until May. Then it leads down to Espley, the hamlet I told you about. But the slopes are slippery from the rain already, and I don't want to go back up there. And with your shoes…"

"No good." I marched back to the platform, where the plastic box provided a semblance of shelter. I tried to think while the wind accelerated, howled, chilled my bare thighs.

Steve stood with his arms folded across his chest, staring along the railway line as if expecting a miracle train to appear.

At the end of the platform, the tunnel gaped dark like a hungry mouth.

I had a brainwave. "The tunnel! We'll walk through the tunnel. It's dry in there. And if it's only a mile, as you say, it will be quicker than the road."

"No!" Steve shook his head vehemently. "The road is safer."

"For you, maybe, but not for me. You're a walker, I'm not. Even if I don't drop with exhaustion on the way, it'll take me five hours, and by then it'll be dark. But we'll be through the tunnel in half an hour." I was getting excited by the idea. It was the perfect solution. "Then I'll find somewhere in the hamlet to make a phone call. If you don't want to come, suit yourself."

Cautiously, I stepped down on the track.

I used the wooden sleepers for walking - one step, one sleeper. Only the occasional rock made it a bit difficult. Before me, the tunnel loomed huge; a black picture in an arched, stony frame.

"Don't go there, Allie!" Steve shouted after me. "There might be trains."

But I knew there were no trains on weekends – hadn't the timetable confirmed that? -, and I ignored him. The closer I got to the tunnel, the weaker my resolution grew. The thought of total darkness constricted my throat, but I did not allow hesitation to blow away my courage.

Stalking from sleeper to sleeper, I entered the gaping hole. Above my head, a flock of birds screeched and fluttered to the exit. Then the darkness enveloped me.

For a while, I could still make out the wooden sleepers on the ground, and I strode on steadily. The absence of wind created a weird stillness, not just silence, but a void.

A faint whiff of coal smoke hung in the air, and from time to time, something small scurried past at ground level. Rats? Sleeper to sleeper, I marched on. The darkness became absolute.

Then I heard heavy steps and panting behind me. So Steve was following me after all. "Faster, walk faster," he urged me, his voice hoarse in the darkness.

But already my calves were aching from the walking with such big steps, the balls of my feet hurt, and it was only with utmost concentration that I managed to find a sleeper for every step.

Sleeper, sleeper, sleeper, sleeper. Left, right, left, right. Somewhere, water dripped like from a leaking tap. The air grew damp, adding the odour of moss and lichen to the smell of soot. The dampness crept over my skin. It was an itchy kind of damp, not like the clean rain outside, but a salty blend of stagnant water, sooty fumes and sweat.

If only I hadn't left the safety of the car. Those motorbikes had been yawnishly dull, but right now I wished I was in a warm, well-lit showroom.

"You shouldn't walk on the sleepers," Steve said. "It's dangerous. Walk along the wall."

"That's all right for you, you're wearing trainers. But I have heels. You want to go faster, you walk on." Although I was glad not to be alone in this spooky tunnel, I disliked Steve. I had enough of his patronising talk and chose to ignore him. I gritted my teeth and kept walking.

But he wouldn't be ignored. His big hand gripped my arm. "Walk along the wall. The ground is flat there."

I pulled myself free, my wishing he hadn't followed me into the tunnel. Suspicion gnawed.

With a hot flush, I remembered displaying the contents of my purse. The man might plan to rob me. My thoughts raced through defence options. I could pick up one of the stones on the track, or use my keys to gouge out him eyes. That's what a paperback heroine would do. But I was clumsy even when I wasn't half-lamed by fear. Wobbling on my heels, and without a clue about combat, I'd have no chance against someone as tall and athletic as this man.

If attacked, I would surrender. After all, what was money? Perhaps I should offer to give him my purse now to get it behind me.

Then I told myself to be sensible. The guy hadn't attacked me yet; my imagination was overwrought because of the damp and the dark.

Steve was probably local, because he knew of the hamlet on the other end of the tunnel. He'd gone for a challenging walk across the hill, got caught by the bad weather, and decided to take the train back. Only there was no train.

I stopped my steps. This made no sense.

Steve had known there was no road traffic on Saturdays. He'd even known the telephone was destroyed. How come he didn't know there were no trains on weekends?

He had appeared on the scene after me, and had entered the tunnel after me - a predator pursuing a target.

An animal howled in the distance, like an owl mocking my stupidity. My scalp prickled. I had to get away.

Too late. Strong arms clutched me and pushed me off the track.

"If you want my money, you can have it," I croaked.

"I don't want your money," he growled. He dragged me onwards. "Just a little further. There's a track-checker's recess."

Fear squeezed the breath from my lungs. I struggled to get free, but was slammed against the wall. The stranger's body pressed against mine, suffocating, hot, merciless.

The rails sang.

"The train," he hissed.

"But there are no –" I started, when the air pressure built up. Wind brushed my legs.

Still seeing nothing but darkness, I could hear the locomotive's heavy breath panting from where they'd just come from. In the distance, three tiny dots like glowing pinheads. I could sense its size – a huge monster. Coal smoke filled the air. I clutched at Steve's arms. I heard our combined breaths, panting with exertion and fear. The man seemed as frightened as I was. Then there was the sizzling, swishing, scraping of metal on metal.

A moment later, the monster was upon us, its presence pressing the air from the human lungs. High above their heads, sparks and flames flew, briefly illuminating the driver's cabin, the stoker's silhouette. The rest of the locomotive was black and huge.

Unable to move, I remained pinned to the stone wall. The moment drew out, as if the train meant to keep us captive forever. I gasped for air. Smoke filled my lungs. I didn't dare to cough.

At last, the engine rattled on, pulling in its wake invisible carriages. Only the whining, hissing, clacking sounds of wheels on rails, and the continued pressure of air revealed their presence. Ghastly clusters of sparks exploded like ground level fireworks.

Then it was over. The wind subsided. The train was gone.

I was shaking all over. I ought to say something to Steve, thank him somehow, but no coherent thoughts would form. I stumbled on, towards the growing dot of light that signalled the tunnel's exit and the end of our ordeal.

Howling, water-heavy wind lashed at us when they neared the exit. Rain bit like nails. With gestures, Steve urged me to hurry. I obeyed mutely.

In the shelter of a track-side building, he paused and shouted to make his voice heard above the wind. "This is Espley. Down there's the Old Crown. It's open. You can phone from there."

"Aren't you coming?" The words had to struggle to form in my soot-sore throat.

"No." He pointed to the steep-gabled stone house beside the track. "I live just here. Bye."

I made it into the hot, cigar-smoked pub, where I ordered a hot coffee and used the change to ring Tony.

"I'm so glad you rang. Are you safe?" His concern felt like a warm hug. "Where are you, Allie? I've been so worried; the salesman at the Harley

Davidson shop told me there are no trains on a Sunday. I even drove back to the train stop. Did you get a lift?"

Warm relief washed over me. I asked him to pick me up from the Old Crown in Espley, and promised to tell him the whole story later.

The woman behind the bar was polishing beer tankards. "What happened to you, dear?" Her voice sounded motherly. "Did you get lost in the woods?"

"No – I've come through the tunnel. I meant to get a train but –"

"You shouldn't have, dear. The tunnel is dangerous: they run empty trains on the line sometimes. Only last year, there was a terrible accident."

"Yes, a train did come, but we waited it out in a track checker's recess. A man called Steve was with me." I resolved to send Steve a thank-you card. "Would you know his surname? Tall guy, twenty-one or twenty-two, I guess, lives in the house with the flowers carved on the shutters."

The woman put the tankard down with a clank. "Steve took a shortcut through the tunnel a year ago. Got run over by an unscheduled steam train…"

That's when I decided I absolutely loved motorbikes.

ONLY A FOOL *by Rayne Hall*

The *clack-clack-clack* of your heels echoes through the night-empty street. The drizzle paints needle-streaks in the light of the fake Victorian lamps. Already, the pavement grows slippery with roadside rubbish, rain and rotten leaves. You should have called a taxi while you had the chance. Now it's too late. Around here, the payphones are vandalised.

You stop to consult your *London A-Z* in a street-lamp's jaundiced glow, bending low to shelter the pages from the rain. The map suggests a shortcut. If you turn left into that alley, zigzag through the lanes, cut across the wasteland, you'll get home in under an hour.

Once you walked past that waste ground in daylight, and didn't like it. At night, you'll like it even less, but the drizzle thickens and creeps into the toes of your patent shoes. Why did you have to stay on at the party until after the last bus? Stupid woman. Better get home now, fast.

You dip into the gap between the dark façades. The alley smells of rotten fruit and piss. Two shattered windows wink.

Darkness folds around you.

Steps follow behind you in soft squeaks. When you glance over your shoulder, a figure squeezes against a wall, as if hiding from your sight.

You're a fool. Only a fool parties until after the last bus. Only a fool hesitates over the cab fare. Only a fool reveals ignorance by looking at a map. Only a fool walks alone into an unlit alley.

Fool, fool, fool.

You walk faster. Your heels echo louder, and your heart hammers in your ears. *Da-boom, da-boom, daboom-daboom-daboom.*

Your pursuer's squeaking steps resume, get closer.

You're too stupid to live alone. Didn't Paul tell you so? You should have listened to him, fool.

Keeping your stride, you grope through the tissues and tampons at the bottom of your bag, searching. Only a fool carries her personal alarm out of instant reach.

Men always scent the victim smell about you. Lovers and strangers alike, they home in on you like wolves on easy prey.

Paul used to beat you, bruise you, break you. He told you that, despite your protests, you really enjoyed it.

Only a fool would have put up with it for seven years.

Seven years of fearing your husband's touch. Seven years of shuddering in meek endurance. If only you could have turned tables just once, let him taste the horror and the pain. But a nice girl doesn't fight, and a good woman keeps her mouth shut. Then the discovery of the catalogue, of the items he had marked: The nipple clamps, the torture racks, the chain floggers with skin-tearing hooks. Knowing he planned to use them on you.

Escaping that marriage left you without a protector, vulnerable. Paul would not have let you go out alone at night. With him, you would not have walked into this trap.

Walk faster, now. Take bigger strides. Out-march the imagined danger.

Your arm is grabbed. You're slammed against the wall. Hard. Both hands pinned above your head.

A pimpled face leers down at you. Young. His breath smells of mint and beer. Your pulse pounds, and your tongue tastes fear.

When you squirm in his grip, rough brick chafes your wrists.

His thigh presses against yours. A knife at your throat, its edge a cold line across your neck. "Don't move."

You squeeze against the wall, into it, to get a fraction further away from the knife. Why did you not sign up for that self-defence class?

"Now pull up your skirt. Take your tights off. Your knickers." The attacker pants. "But slow. Or I'll cut."

"No," your voice croaks, from far away. Then, stronger: "No. You wouldn't like my kind of sex."

Where did those words come from?

The edge leaves your throat. The grip on your wrists slackens a little.

Perhaps your attacker is not a seasoned rapist. Perhaps he's a boy trying it out. If you play this right, you may get away.

Perhaps.

"What kind of sex?" His eyes glint. "Why wouldn't I like it?"

You search your fear-paralysed brain for the reply that will buy time. "Few men have what it takes to please me."

For three heartbeats, his mouth stays open. Then a tongue wipes his lip. "Really?"

The grip around your wrist loosens more. The blade rests inches away from your throat. What caused this change? How can you use it?

His grin widens. "I knew you were different from others the first time I saw you." Leer. "A dominatrix. With leather gear and whip?"

Scheherazade used to spin yarns to save her life. Improvise. Quick.

"I wear black boots. Shiny patent leather. They reach up to here..." You expect him to release your hands so you can show, but he doesn't. Keep talking anyway. "Up to my thighs. With very high spiky heels."

He leans closer again, licks his lips. "What kind of whip?"

Paul's catalogue. The images. Remember. "Black suede. Thirteen long lashes. A plaited handle with silver studs. It sings and sizzles through the air before it thuds on your skin. Then there's a sharp sting..." The fantasy comes surprisingly easy. "But I don't sully my precious flogger on a dirty boy like you."

"Hey, why not?" He steps back. "Just because…"

"Precisely. Because." Your hands are free now. But to be safe, you must not run yet, must play the role a moment longer. "You don't deserve it. You have not earned the kiss of my whip. Nor the…" Scan your memory for images from the hateful catalogue. "The dog collar, the handcuffs, the cane…"

"The whip. Please." His eyes gleam with need and hope. "Let your whip kiss my arse. I'll be good."

Can this change be true? The pleasure of power tingles from your fingertips to your toes, invigorating every cell of your flesh. The strong animal in you, suppressed for so long, longs to burst from its cage. No longer a passive victim, now you can be in charge.

Purse your lips, as if assessing his potential. "If I give you a chance to redeem yourself, will you show me respect? Will you obey my will?"

"Yes, yes! " The eager face of a dog begging for crumbs.

"Then…" You stab a finger at his chest. "You will stay here, waiting, while I fetch my lovely, leathery whip. I'll test you, and if you're good, I'll let you feel its caress."

The pimply face lights. "I know a great place where we can go, not far from here. Behind the old cable factory. Nobody ever goes there."

Time for a stern frown. "It is I who choose the place."

"I go where you command."

"Stay here. Practice kneeling. Because when I come back, you'll be kneeling a lot."

Before the fool sees he's been duped, you stride off with power in your steps.

Your blood pulses. You're safe, and fuelled with new power. You've taken charge. No longer the victim. No longer the fool.

Of course you will not come back.

Why should you? Just to get another taste of this tingling power surge? Just to teach this boy a lesson that all males should learn? Just to punish him for all the abuse you had to suffer from men?

There's rage pounding through you, too. Rage at Paul who abused you for years. Rage at men who attack women in the street. Rage at men who treat you as a fool.

The boy will be waiting. At your mercy. He'll go where you want, even to that deserted waste ground, and better still, to that place where nobody ever goes. He'll undress at your command, he'll kneel, he'll hold up his hands to be tied and open his mouth to take the gag.

Is this what Paul felt, this lust to hurt? It feels surprisingly good. The long-suppressed part of you cracks its chrysalis.

What will it feel like to slice a knife into those pale cheeks? To peel off his skin. To let his warm blood trickle over your hands. How soon will the scents of blood and fear outgrow those of beer and mint? To see the fear in his eyes. Uncertainty first. Then fright. Panic. Terror. Knowledge of death.

Will you give him what he deserves? What all men deserve.

Nobody knows who he is going to meet, so his body, when finally found, won't be linked to you. He's the perfect first object for your vengeance.

Only a fool would let this chance pass by.

DEAR READER

I hope you've enjoyed this book and gained many practical ideas for your writing. If you found it helpful, I'll be thrilled if you post a review on Amazon, Barnes&Noble, GoodReads, or wherever you purchased it or are a member.

If you email me the URL to your review, I'll send you a review copy of one of my other Writer's Craft books: *Writing Fight Scenes, Writing about Magic, The Word-Loss Diet, Writing About Villains, Writing Dark Stories, Writing Vivid Settings, Twitter for Writers, SWOT for Writing Success, Writing Short Stories To Promote Your Novels, How To Train Your Cat To Promote Your Book, Why Does My Book Not Sell?20 Simple Fixes, Getting Book Reviews, Writing Deep Point of View.* Email me which book you would like to review, *and I'll send it to you free.*

*Let me know if you've found any errors, omissions, broken links or typos in this book, please let me know. Some errors always sneak past the eagle eyes of the proofreaders. Also contact me if you have questions. My email is **raynehall00000@gmail.com**. I look forward to hearing from you.*

Perhaps you know other writers who might benefit from this book? Tell them about it.

On Twitter, you can follow me @RayneHall. https://twitter.com/RayneHall I'm very active on Twitter; it's my preferred social network. If you tweet that you've read this book, I'll follow you back – though you may have to remind me, because I have many followers and it's easy to miss a tweet.

My website is here: raynehallauthor.wix.com/rayne-hall.

Rayne Hall

Made in the USA
Middletown, DE
02 September 2023